FAVOURITE HOLES BY DESIGN

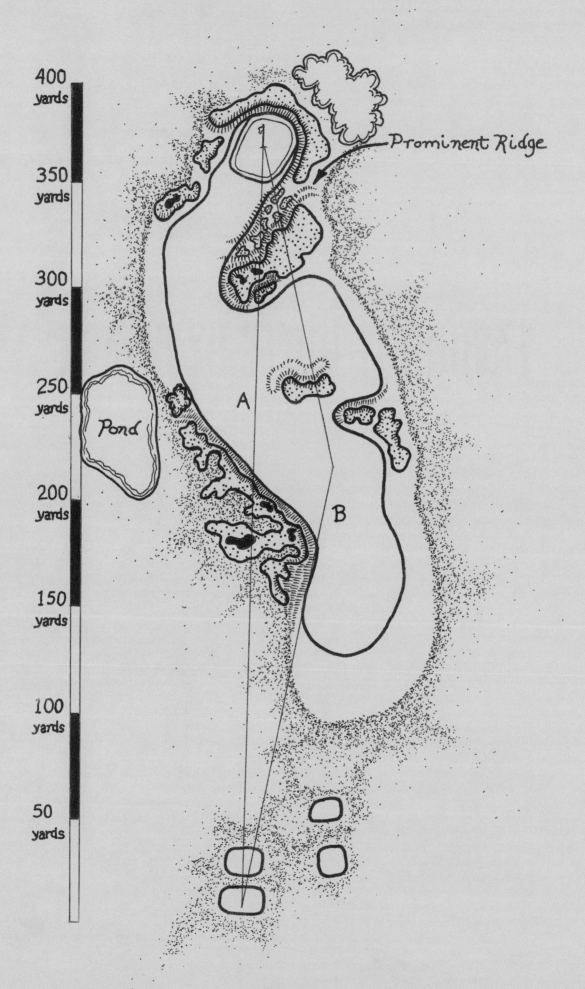

400 yards

350 yards

300 yards

250 yards

Pond

200 yards

150 yards

100 yards

50 yards

Prominent Ridge

A

B

FAVOURITE HOLES BY DESIGN

THE ARCHITECT'S CHOICE   PAUL DALEY

FULL SWING GOLF PUBLISHING

First published in 2004
by Full Swing Golf Publishing
P.O. Box 1187
Glen Waverley
Victoria 3150 Australia

National Library of Australia Cataloguing-in-Publication Data:
  Daley, Paul

Favourite holes by design : the architect's choice.

  ISBN 0 9581363 2 7.

  1. Golf courses. 2. Golf courses – Design and construction.

  3. Golf courses – Pictorial works. I. Title.

796.352068

Cover and text design by Andrew Cunningham – Studio Pazzo.
Typesetting and layout by Andrew Cunningham – Studio Pazzo.
Produced in China through Bookbuilders.

Note

Each essay is accompanied by 'boxed' information pertaining to the featured hole.
The year of design denotes when *that* particular hole was designed, not necessarily
when the course was designed, or, when the golf course was opened for play. While
the architect of record listed is weighted toward who designed *that* particular hole,
in many instances, that person also designed the course.

Throughout the book, all references to hole and course lengths will be consistent with
the system of measurement of that country. American courses use the imperial
system, while European and Commonwealth courses use the metric system.

Royal Troon Golf Club: Eighth hole, Scotland.
(Photo by Larry Lambrecht, LC Lambrecht Photography.)

Contents

Introduction
Paul Daley

Golf architects encounter many thousands of golf holes in their chosen profession, so it is of interest when they elevate one hole above all others. Pinpointing exactly how this occurs is beyond the scope of this book, yet readers will no doubt speculate. Perhaps a hole makes its mark by simply fitting the architect's eye, or by reflecting a long-held design philosophy. It may also represent the type of hole that its author has fantasised about designing should similar terrain, conditions, and an adequate budget present. But this is purely academic. A few architects politely declined to participate in the project—their minds too full of 'favourites.'

The brief to architects was simple: select your favourite hole, not what you consider to be the best. Surely there will be an overlap: some degree of overlap is entirely natural and predictable. Answering the call in good faith, architects have abstained from writing about a hole that they, or their firm, have designed.

Many of the iconic golf holes of the world are included in *Favourite Holes*, but less-heralded entries have their supporters. Courtesy of US architect, Kyle Phillips, we learn of Harry S. Colt's visit to The Netherlands where he designed a gem of a hole and course. Five-times Open Champion, James Braid, was a wonderful and prolific designer of golf courses. With due admiration, Welsh architect, Ian Scott-Taylor details Braid's sporty, bunkerless opening hole at Holyhead, Wales. And England's Royal Worlington and Newmarket—long regarded by aficionados as possibly the finest nine-hole layout in the world—scores a welcome entry. Unaccountably, this Suffolk layout remains largely unknown to the wider golfing community. English architect, Martin Ebert, fell under the spell of its fifth hole long ago, and outlines its merit in great detail. A golf hole called 'Donga?' The Australian country town of Mudgee in the State of New South Wales is where you'll find it, and Australian architect, James Wilcher, explains its various charms and difficulties. US architect Ronald Fream has nominated the fourth hole at the Himalayan Golf Club, Nepal. Many would be unaware that our great game had even spread that far!

A golfer's favourite hole can change over time. In my own case as a boy of ten, I played up and down the Apollo Bay foreshore, fashioning a seven-iron over its precinct before school and getting hooked on the game. In the downwind direction it took two seven-iron's to find my imaginary target, while four 'gut-buster's' were required heading back into the wind, to find another. Well before the Reverse Course at St. Andrews had seeped into my consciousness, I had my own Reverse Apollo Bay foreshore! But how my 'hole' has changed: the area now resembles a commercialised obstacle course. Barely five years later, the Apollo Bay foreshore was supplanted by another western-Victoria hole: a real one—the short, par-four sixth hole at Cobden over 'Snake' creek. With no disrespect to the virtues of Cobden's sixth, it has since been replaced by the sixth hole on the West Course at Royal Melbourne. And there it will stay. US architect Forrest Richardson saw no need to go beyond a favourite hole from his youth. Indeed, Forrest has nominated a hole that no longer exists: the defunct fifteenth hole at The Valley Club, Phoenix, designed by David Gill in 1957.

Golf enthusiasts are progressively thirsting for golf lists. In recognition of this fact, the endmatter features a list of each contributor's fifteen favourite holes. Five entries of each par-type are nominated, and it is fascinating to observe which holes continually reappear. I do hope you enjoy *Favourite Holes by Design: The Architect's Choice*.

Banff Springs Golf Club: Fourth hole, Canada.
(Photo by Aidan Bradley, Aidan Bradley Photography.)

Oakmont Country Club, USA
Eighteenth hole Jack Snyder

I've always reserved a soft spot in my heart for Oakmont Country Club. The family ties are strong, dating back to 1907 when my father, Arthur Armstrong Snyder, began caddying at this great club. Eventually, he became the personal caddie of W. C. Fownes Jr., who was an acclaimed amateur player and the son of Oakmont's founder, Henry C. Fownes. In time, dad worked on the ground staff at Oakmont and eventually became the green-keeper at Alcoma Country Club, another private club in Pittsburgh. This led to my life in golf, as it did for both of my brothers, Jim and Carl. We all became golf-course superintendents, and it was only later that I ventured into designing golf courses.

Few realised that Henry C. Fownes routed Oakmont simply by placing stakes in the ground in positions he felt best represented tees, angle points, and greens. Fownes, who owned the property, thought of the course as a hobby. As it was passed down from generation to generation, each next of kin made improvements to the course and took pride in making it more difficult—very difficult indeed. The entire philosophy at Oakmont was to tweak the design as often as necessary in order to keep it as a defining test of golf. That philosophy remains in vogue today.

I graduated from Penn State University in 1939 with a degree in Landscape Architecture, and the following year I started a business in landscape architectural design and construction in the Pittsburgh area. After being interrupted by World War II—during which I designed rocket projectiles and worked on other defense projects—I returned to my landscape design business. Fortuitously, one of my clients was none other than John Jackson, President of Oakmont Country Club.

Due to my previous turfgrass experience and LA qualification, John suggested that I be retained as Superintendent of Grounds at Oakmont. When I accepted the position in the early 1950s, it was my job to maintain the great traditions, and direct some changes to the design, notably, the eighth green, which is such a rich part of the Oakmont legacy. At this period in time, the course was being negatively impacted by construction of the Pennsylvania Turnpike. The road was being built at a depressed elevation through the golf course, and it presented a number of challenges.

Considering my close association with Oakmont, it is difficult to choose a favourite hole. Over the years, its design has been fine-tuned to ensure that the challenge remains relevant for even the most skilled golfer. Nearly every hole requires the average golfer to hit a solid drive down the middle, followed by a long-iron approach to the green.

Oakmont's famous ditches were designed originally as hazards, while any drainage provided by them was welcomed and viewed as a bonus. Sand traps were deep and rugged. Years ago, each one was maintained by furrowed rakes, and such was their design that it occasionally mandated a lateral escape by the golfer. And, as if these elements weren't difficult enough, the greens have always been hard and fast.

I am so fond of all the holes at Oakmont that to be perfectly honest, it's almost too difficult to name a true favourite. However, if there has been one hole guaranteed to put a smile on my face, I couldn't go past the par-four, eighteenth hole. During the writing of this piece, it forced me to examine what makes this hole so special. Well, I will admit that whenever I played the hole, I realised that my pain and suffering was soon to be over! Even when visiting the course in 2003, the same emotion generated by the eighteenth

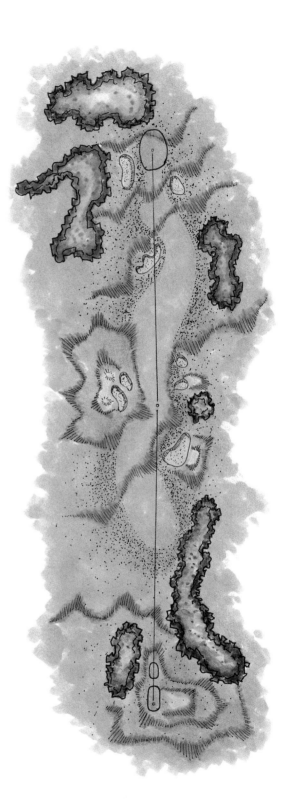

hole came flooding back. I recall many times how I had longed to see that majestic clubhouse: the backdrop to the difficult and long approach to this well-trapped green.

The eighteenth has all the elements required of an inspiring, finishing hole. It is an extremely difficult par-four between 412 and 430 yards in length, demanding a long drive down the centre of the fairway, followed by a long, accurate second shot. You guessed it: like every other par-four at Oakmont Country Club!

The view from the tee is simply spectacular, and I've never grown tired of it. The fairway is lined with mature trees, and behind the green is that wonderful old clubhouse. The tee-shot must thread the needle between five sand traps, to a narrow landing area that slopes from left to right. The green is elevated and flanked by a trap on each side, and another one resides sixty-five yards short of the green—just for good measure.

The eighteenth green can be nightmarishly quick, and it slopes from back to front. Any downhill putt from above the pin is almost destined to be a three-putt encounter, that is, unless your first putt hits the hole. From time to time, a golfer will conquer Oakmont's eighteenth hole and the feeling is one of sheer elation, knowing full well that here is one of the greatest—if not the greatest—finishing hole in golf. Escaping with a fortunate par, or perhaps scoring a fine birdie, tops off a really great day. Unfortunately, though, I cannot recall too many times when I managed that!

Forrest Richardson & Associates
Golf Course Architects,
Phoenix, Arizona, USA

Note: I've used the term 'sand trap' instead of 'bunker' because in the true dialect of Western Pennsylvania it has always been 'sand trap.' That's what we called them, and that's how my father described them when he was working alongside the Fownes' during Oakmont's early days, when so many design changes took place at the course.

Par-4
MEN'S: 456 Yards
WOMEN'S: 415 Yards (Par-5)
DESIGNER: Henry C. Fownes (1903)

Ballybunion Golf Club, Ireland

Fifteenth hole: Cashen Course Robin Hiseman

Isn't it great when something not only meets your expectations, but exceeds them. Especially when your expectations were so high to begin with. That pretty much sums up my experiences at Ballybunion, which are nothing short of the best times I have ever had on a golf course.

When it came to choosing a favourite hole it was not too difficult to narrow it down to one from this fabulous Irish links, but to find the one that had ingrained itself as surpassing all others was not so straightforward. In the end, after scanning through the four and a half thousand other holes I've played, I have nominated the one that exerts the most profound emotional effect upon me. That hole is the par-five, fifteenth on Ballybunion's Cashen Course, which left me slack-jawed in astonishment when I first saw it.

Supposedly, I should demonstrate an appreciation for my profession by choosing a design of fabulous strategic intricacy, which I can then expertly dissect to show you how clever I am. But this hole prevents me from doing that, because it doesn't really have an apparent playing strategy. Its defences are physical: it has some of the most immense and extreme dune terrain to be found anywhere on the planet, and it is definitely a candidate for the most spectacular hole ever created. Even so, I do acknowledge that as an example of strategic golf course architecture, it is fundamentally flawed.

The tiny green is hoisted high up the side of a vast sand dune, with steep, broken ground, and a filled-in bunker protecting the approach. It is practically impossible to keep an approach shot on this green with anything less than a perfectly lofted wedge.

To comprehend the fifteenth hole, and the Cashen Course as a whole, you do need to approach it with a spirit of adventure. This is raw, aggressive golf—a severe test of nerve, patience and physical endurance.

It makes no pretence to be fair, but as an example of layout planning, it is pure genius.

I can only imagine how exciting it must have been for Robert Trent Jones and Cabell Robinson to first discover these towering, cathedral-like dunes, with the thought of laying a golf hole through them. When I rounded the dogleg and set eyes upon the distant green for the first time, I remember my exact response: 'Wow!' And I repeated that word many times. I felt like the first explorer to discover the lost city of Petra, for the scene before me was almost mystical in its magnificence. A single shaft of late-evening sunlight flooded the tiny, pulpit green, while all else lay in sinister, dark shadows cast by the gigantic dunes. The soft breeze died and the constant cymbal crash of the Atlantic breakers faded away to an eerie silence as we descended the cascading fairway, into a cavernous hollow encircled by colossal sand hills. A choir of angels sang in chorus, as the shimmering Mother Ship rose slowly from behind the sixteenth tee. [All right, I made up that last bit, but it would have only been marginally more dramatic.] This didn't feel like recreation, this was a 'close encounter of the golfing kind.'

Just sometimes, you find yourself in exactly the right mood to fully absorb and appreciate the moment. Back in May 1993, taking in the riot of sensory experiences, which reached a crescendo standing in fifteenth fairway, I was overwhelmed with feelings of awe, excitement and anticipation. Above all, there was the surge of pure joy to be a golfer and to have the opportunity to experience such a wondrous landscape while playing the game I love. For those few minutes it existed just for us, and nobody else. They were perfect moments.

Robin Hiseman Golf Course Design
Laurencekirk, Kincardineshire, Scotland

HOLE 15 CASHEN COURSE, BALLYBUNION

MLH '04

Par-5
MEN'S: 487 Yards
WOMEN'S: 393 Yards
DESIGNER: Robert Trent Jones Sr. (1980)

Royal Adelaide Golf Club, Australia
Third hole Neil Crafter

The Adelaide Golf Club moved to its present seaside Seaton site in 1904, yet its boldest move came in 1926 when the Club invited Dr Alister Mackenzie to advise on modifications to its layout. After visiting the course twice in October and November 1926, he quickly recognised the cumbersome aspect of playing across the Adelaide-to- Grange railway line that bisected the course. That silliness was removed! A further consequence of Mackenzie's revised routing was acknowledgment of the under-utilisation of the natural sand dunes and sand craters in the site. That, too, became a thing of the past.

The land occupied by Royal Adelaide's current third hole is very sandy and was not used by Swift and Rymill in their 1906 'permanent' layout. Mackenzie's eye for 'golf country' enabled the identification of a short par-four in this vacant area of the property—one destined to be a classic. As is often the case, one change has a ripple effect; it allowed the tee-shot at the new fourth hole to carry a huge sand crater—one that had also been ignored until that time. The Doctor was smitten with this part of the property and arranged for a photographer to take some pictures for him. The crater at the fourth, and the site for the new third green featured in his articles in UK *Golf Illustrated* (1927) on his Australian tour. Interestingly, Mackenzie's plan for the remodelling of the Royal Adelaide course showed two greenside bunkers: one at front right; and one at middle-left of a diamond-shaped green. These were never built, while the green is much longer and narrower than the one Mackenzie envisaged.

Unfortunately, his written report to the Club has since been lost; much of what we know about his visit comes from press reports of the period. In August 1928, some eighteen months after the Club's adoption of Mackenzie's plan, the Adelaide *Register* published an article by committeeman, J. L. Lewis. Describing the alterations to the third hole, he wrote:

Hole 3 will be played from a tee between the present 18th green and the railway line, to a beautifully placed leg of mutton green in the crater going to the present eleventh. This hole, although only 300 yards, will call for two very accurate shots. It is distinctly 'a hole of class.'

The article draws no reference to any bunkers, despite the prominence of these on Mackenzie's drawing; the idea of including them appears to have been abandoned after Mackenzie left Australia. Whoever was responsible for this decision made a choice of sheer architectural genius, most probably without realising it.

Enough of the pre-amble: why have I selected this as my favourite hole in golf? It showcases the perfect marriage where the simple concept of the great, short par-four, combines with a marvellous natural piece of land unreliant upon artificial hazards for its challenge. On such a stage, eagles and double bogeys are both likely, yet so is any score in between. And isn't that half the fun! Royal Adelaide's third hole introduces golfers to the sand dune country, following the relative flatness of the opening two holes. The natural dunes land provides all the necessary golfing elements needed for a wonderfully compact two-shotter, without the use of a single bunker. All that was required was the building of a tee and a green—the rest was left to nature.

From a tee perched on the side of the railway line, golfers must be unequivocal about their tee-shot strategy. Prudent play may see golfers opting for a three-iron to the top of the ridge that traverses the fairway. Assuming success, there is still much to do: leaving a tricky wedge shot into a long and narrow green that is slightly angled across the line of play, from back-left, to front-right. The green is set down on the floor of a broad, dune valley and is guarded on its left-hand side by a steep and narrow embankment. This is covered by heavy rough and set diagonally to the line of play. Examination of the photograph of this greensite taken for Mackenzie shows that this bank was an existing natural linear dune feature, and it was covered in reeds. A sharp, grassy knob intrudes to the edge of the green from the towering dune that extends down the right side of the hole. These dunes are covered by reeds, marram grasses, as well as pine trees, and are matched by smaller dunes down the left of the fairway. Combined, these features form a fearsome rough.

For golfers who insist upon gambling with a driver, the third green is reachable, but they will be flying 'blind' from the tee. As the fairway beyond the ridge slopes from right to left down from the dunes, the drive must be threaded precisely down the right edge of the fairway in order to receive a favourable kick toward the green's opening. As Norman von Nida would testify, the hole has real teeth: he took a nine here once to lose the Australian Open. For shorter hitters unable to reach the crest of the ridge, the approach shot is also blind, but a short walk to the top will enable them to survey what lies ahead.

The tee-shot that clears the ridge without enough impetus to reach the flat, will remain on the downslope. What follows is the most awkward sixty-metre pitch shot on the entire course. And this especially applies if the pin is tucked away to the left beyond the embankment. If the pitch shot is feeble, it will get tangled up in the thick rough on the bank; if too bold, a tricky, downhill putt will await. However, the thrill of playing a high pitch to a pin on the left of this green is not to be missed—watching it clear the embankment and hoping that it doesn't either get caught up, or appear too quickly into view is one of those special golfing moments.

The first half of the putting surface is narrow and continues out of the approach at the same level. Golfers will find the back half to be much wider, and it slopes a little more from back to front. The right rear of the green falls off into a shallow, grassy hollow beyond the knob.

There's no doubt: walking off Royal Adelaide's third hole with a birdie puts a spring in one's step to face the testing fourth. A bogey or worse, however, can make the uphill walk to the next tee seem like climbing Mt. Everest.

Many a knowledgeable spectator has gathered atop the dunes alongside the third green during tournaments, awaiting the arrival of bold competitors who may try to drive the green. The golfer will not see if their tee-shot is successful. The response of the crowd on the hill will dutifully inform. Applause will mean success, while silence will indicate that problems have only just begun.

Golf Strategies
Adelaide, South Australia, Australia

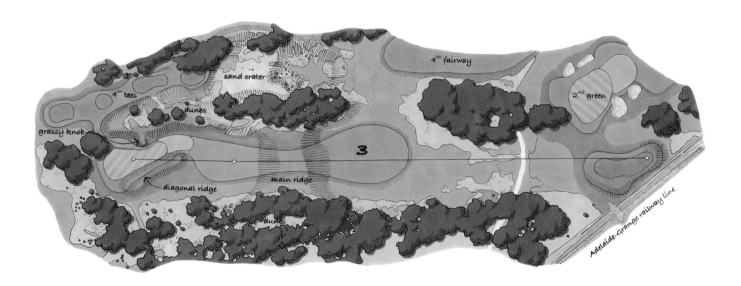

Par-4
MEN'S: **270 Metres**
WOMEN'S: **247 Metres**
DESIGNER: **Alister Mackenzie (1926)**

Ridgewood Country Club, USA

Fourth hole: West Course Gil Hanse

Like every golf-course architect who has ever plied this trade, A. W. Tillinghast was not embarrassed to copy the concept of a golf hole he admired, and then incorporate it into his designs. C. B. Macdonald used the concept of the 'Ideal course' and constantly repeated it with a set of ideal golf holes—many of them borrowed from the links of Britain. And so it was with Tillinghast and the fourth hole at Ridgewood Country Club (West Course) in Ridgewood, New Jersey.

The hole is a spin-off of the seventh hole at Pine Valley, which is home to the awesome hazard: Hell's Half Acre. Those golfers fortunate to have played here will recall how the hazard divides the fairway into two 'safe' and separate entities. As a par-five, Hell's Half Acre is to be carried—hopefully between the first and second shots—and the reward is an opportunity to get home with one's third shot. This hazard places a high premium on both the tee-shot, and the second shot, making for an incredible three-shot hole. In fact, it would be a major surprise should the hole not appear in this book.

Having visited George Crump and Pine Valley during its construction, Tillinghast became enamoured with his friend's creation. Indeed, so enamoured was he with the design of the seventh hole, that he began to take credit for making suggestions to Crump, saying: 'Crump incorporated two of my conceptions entirely'—the long seventh, and the thirteenth hole. Writing further of the true three-shotter, Tillinghast states: 'There must be something along the line which makes one think; something to invite brave endeavour; and a suitable reward for the accomplishment.' He further added: 'the most effectual method, and I believe the only satisfactory one, is the location of a truly formidable hazard across the fairway.' This hole became a staple feature of his designs and can be found at other golf courses, namely, the third hole at Fenway, the fourteenth hole at Quaker Ridge, the seventeenth hole at Baltusrol (Lower Course), and on two holes at Ridgewood Country Club: third hole (East Course); and the fourth hole (West Course).

With this concept being widely used, I have asked myself why the par-five, fourth hole at Ridgewood West so intrigues me, above others, and shines as such a fine example. I have narrowed it down to two main reasons: the combined use of limited visibility; and the golf-course boundary as hazards.

The downhill tee-shot seems straightforward enough, however, a premium is placed on getting the ball sufficiently far enough to make the carry over the barren 'Sahara', bereft of sand. A long, sinewy bunker guards the right-hand side of the hole, which provides the player with the best angle to play to the left with the next shot. From the landing area, it is difficult to view the second-shot area, as one must play over the mounds and then up a slight ridge to where the fairway resumes. The mounding and the fairway are placed on a slight diagonal with the longest carry—down the left-hand side—reaping the greatest reward. In another unique twist to this hole, Tillinghast extended the mounds into the adjacent fairway of the fifth hole on the West Course. The close proximity of this fairway serves as an alternative avenue of play if one deems the carry over the mounds too burdensome.

The so-called 'proper' second shot should be played out to the left, near the Out-of-bounds, which gains the best angle for the third shot into the green. This desirable angle is set up by some dramatic bunkering, which nearly encircles the green, with the narrow opening coming from the left side.

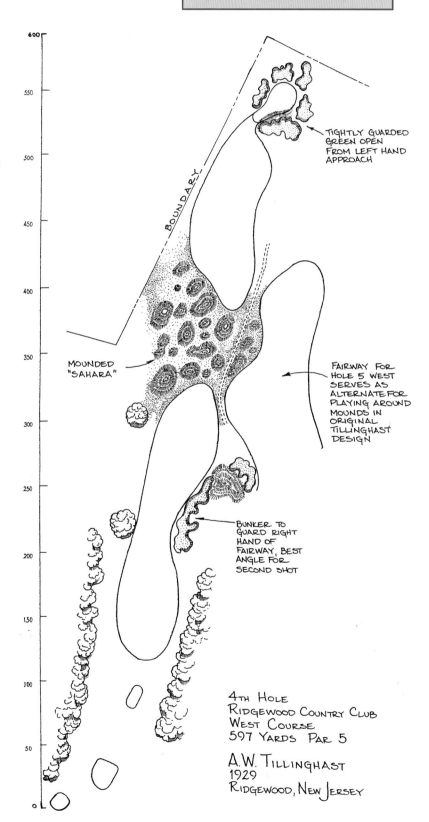

Par-4
MEN'S: 597 Yards
WOMEN'S: 464 Yards
DESIGNER: A. W. Tillinghast (1929)

TIGHTLY GUARDED GREEN OPEN FROM LEFT HAND APPROACH

BOUNDARY

FAIRWAY FOR HOLE 5 WEST SERVES AS ALTERNATE FOR PLAYING AROUND MOUNDS IN ORIGINAL TILLINGHAST DESIGN

MOUNDED "SAHARA"

BUNKER TO GUARD RIGHT HAND OF FAIRWAY, BEST ANGLE FOR SECOND SHOT

4TH HOLE
RIDGEWOOD COUNTRY CLUB
WEST COURSE
597 YARDS PAR 5

A.W. TILLINGHAST
1929
RIDGEWOOD, NEW JERSEY

The green, itself, is unforgettable in shape: a long, narrow neck widening out to a bigger bowl in the back of the green. The strong slope that feeds off the right-front bunker makes approach shots from the right more difficult to 'stick' on the green. Even when a golfer's ball finds the green, there is still much work to do, as the strong slope in the green can make putting an adventure.

To conclude this piece, I find it invigorating to see the use of cross-hazards and boundaries as integral and legitimate design strategy. I say this from a golfer's point of view, but also with my architect's hat on. In this era of concerns over liability and fairness, it is always good for the soul to see examples of holes that are bold and imaginative. The fourth hole at Ridgewood is one such hole that offers a treasure trove of playing options, and it provides golfers with an opportunity to 'tack' from side-to-side to gain the advantage. Perhaps more than any other element, Tillinghast's design brings out what is essential to the success of any par-five: a second shot that is loaded with drama, purpose, and excitement.

Hanse Golf Course Design, Inc.
Malvern, Pennsylvania, USA

The Wentworth Club, England
Eleventh hole: West Course Tim Lobb

For the golfer standing on the eleventh tee on Wentworth's West Course, no more pertinent words could ring so true as those uttered by Henry Cotton, the great English professional of yesteryear. He quipped: 'the indescribable joy of driving downhill.' This pleasure is heightened by a number of factors: the elevated tee-shot over bracken and heather; the awaiting fairway, which is located within a natural valley; and the trees, which border the slender fairway ahead. Standing on high, all the elements fuse together to provide an exhilarating golfing experience.

Course designer, and ex-Sunningdale secretary, Harry S. Colt, designed the West Course in 1926, with its construction completed the following year. The club was the brainchild of property developer, Walter Tarrant, who in 1920 purchased 1750 acres of woodland/heathland for £42,000. Wentworth is located in Virginia Water—around twenty miles west of London, and near Ascot in Surrey—and Tarrant's vision was to select Colt to help create a luxurious country club, and combine it with an opulent housing development. History has vindicated this selection, repeatedly, for Colt was an architect of pedigree. During World War II, German prisoners of war from a camp nearby, in Egham, were brought in to clear the overgrown vegetation that had proliferated on the last six holes during the West's wartime closure. The course was aptly named the 'Burma Road.'

Much of Wentworth's notoriety can be attributed to the club hosting important and well-publicised tournaments. Among them: the Ryder Cup in 1926 and 1953; the Curtis Cup in 1932; and the Canada Cup in 1956—now known as the World Cup. It was this latter event that marked Ben Hogan's second, and last, appearance in Britain. Indeed, the Ryder Cup grew out of an informal match between Americans and Britons in 1926 over Wentworth's (East) Course. Bobby Jones was in irresistible form: returning an impeccable round of sixty-six, containing thirty-three shots and thirty-three putts. Jones went out in thirty-three, and came home in the same score, prompting many at the time to assess it as the finest round of all-time. Later in the clubhouse bar, Samuel Ryder remarked: 'We should do this again,' so he donated a trophy and a marvellous golfing tradition—based on formal competition between the US and British teams—was born. Given these circumstances, it is surprising that only once, in 1953, has the Ryder Cup formally been held at Wentworth. But in 1964, when the late Mark McCormack—founder of IMG—created the World Match Play Championship, Wentworth announced itself emphatically on the international golf scene. The major stars and drawcards of the day—Player, Nicklaus, Palmer, and others—frequented the tournament, and the Wentworth story was in full swing.

The par-four, eleventh hole on the West Course follows the difficult par-three tenth, and it requires precise shotmaking to achieve one's goals. As a concession to technological advances in equipment, the building of a championship tee in the late 1990s has seen the addition of twenty-seven yards to the hole. The drive is downhill, to a fairway that sweeps away to the left, bordered by local vegetation. From such elevation, the view is absurdly impressive, being dominated by pine trees, bracken, and heather. The short-iron approach to the green is played through the natural valley, to a noticeably elevated and slightly angled green, which is guarded by three modest greenside bunkers. When approaching the green, an advanced sense for distance-control is of utmost importance, given the golfer's inability to view the bottom of the flagstick from the fairway. Finally, the cleverly

Par–4
MEN'S: **403 Yards**
WOMEN'S: **318 Yards**
DESIGNER: **Harry S. Colt (1926)**

contoured green forms an excellent defence against golfers merely lining up their putts, then holing out. On this green, there is nothing straightforward about putting.

The great South African golfer, Bobby Locke, so adored the eleventh hole on the Burma Road Course, that he included it in his world best eighteen-holes. As a prolific international traveller, and consistent winner, his comment carries considerable weight.

For this writing assignment, I suppose that a more spectacular hole could have been nominated. But when I consider Colt's vision, his precise placement of features and hazards, and the execution of his desired design philosophy, I can see that I'm on solid footing. Colt's finished product has melded beautifully, making it an absolute joy to play this most attractive golf hole.

European Golf Design
Sunningdale, Berkshire, England

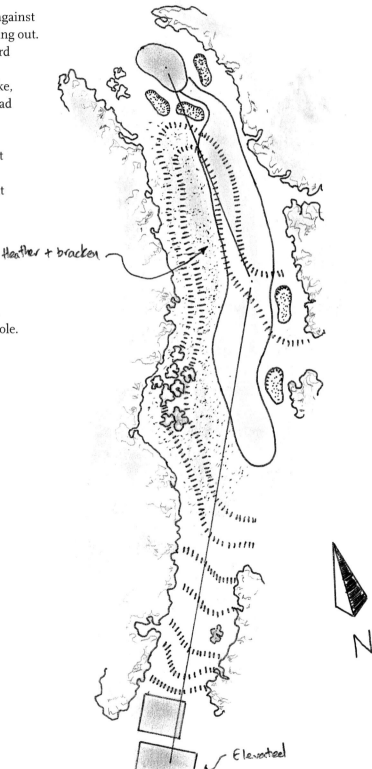

Heather + bracken

Elevated

N

The Gleneagles Hotel, Scotland
Thirteenth hole: King's Course David McLay Kidd

I spent much of my later childhood at Gleneagles in Scotland where my father is the Courses Manager. I could play the lesser known courses—Queens; Princes; and Glendevon—whenever I wished but my father only granted me permission occasionally to play the revered King's Course. I loved playing Braid's masterpiece then and now, although for over the twenty years since I first teed it up, my game has improved, along with the balls and clubs I use. Collectively, this has completely changed my playing strategy on many holes over this layout.

In selecting my favourite hole, I'd have to agree with five-time Open winner and renowned architect from the Golden Age of golf-course design James Braid. The thirteenth hole—originally the fourteenth—on the King's course is aptly named 'Braid's Brawest,' meaning Braid's Greatest. In April 1914, the Caledonian Railway Company appointed Messrs Braid and Hutchinson, agreeing to pay £120 plus expenses for their design services.

My chosen hole is wild and unpredictable, amid the tumbling Perthshire terrain. Like many golf holes from a bygone era, advances in equipment technology have reduced it to a lengthy par-four, rather than the monstrous par-five it was in the 1920s. From the Men's back-tee it's a stretch at 464 yards, and the hole still plays as a par-five from the Women's green tee.

The King's Course at Gleneagles, and especially 'Braid's Brawest,' epitomises much of the great man's golf design philosophy. Short and sweet, it is listed below:

- *Holes should present variety of: length; demands made of the player; style of bunkering; and method of approach.*
- *Putting greens should be well guarded.*
- *The size of the green is governed by the length of approach. The shorter the shot, the smaller the green.*
- *Alternative tees should be provided to enable playing conditions to be adapted to prevailing or contrary winds, dry or wet weather.*
- *The bunkering and general planning of holes should reward good positional play.*
- *Alternative routes should be provided to each hole.*

When standing on the thirteenth tee, you just know you'll have your work cut out to secure par figures. Issues conspire against the golfer: the green falls steeply away from incoming shots—front-right to back-left; there is no approach into the green, making a running approach impossible; and the wind is generally at your back, negating any thought of stopping your ball on the green. There are easier holes!

For a hole approaching its centenary, it is somewhat surprising that almost all the original bunkers remain relevant and in play. A good drive is essential to clear the ridge and thread the bunkers, while one slightly right of centre will normally result in a favourable forward bounce. Any tee-shot to the left will be snared by a bunker known as 'Auld Nick,' but stray a little to the right and another bunker added after Braid's time will claim your ball. Following a bunkered or wayward drive, the player really must reconsider playing the hole as Braid intended—a three-shot hole.

A good drive by the single-figure handicap golfer is rewarded with a relatively flat lie and playable shot of 180 to 190 yards to the green. Canny 'local' knowledge dictates that you aim your approach to the right of the pin, allowing the slope of the green to work the ball down to the pin.

'Braid's Brawest'
Par-4
MEN'S: 464 Yards
WOMEN'S: 418 Yards (Par-5)
DESIGNER: James Braid (1926)

Weak shots invariably find the greenside bunker 'Young Nick,' whereas bold play has its own glorious reward: a ball situated behind the pin, leaving an uphill birdie putt.

For golfers who choose, or are forced, to lay-up their approach with a short to mid-iron, they will find their ball in a deep hollow in front of the green. This position leaves a short but 'blind' wedge.

As an avid golfer and golf architect, I love the challenge of utilising the contour of a golf hole in the strategy. Target golf is one-dimensional and contrary to the very essence of the game.

DMK Golf Design Limited
Heybridge, Essex, England

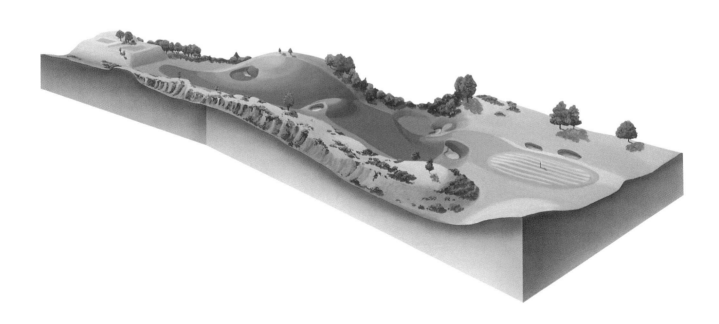

St. Andrews, Scotland
Second hole: The Old Course Tom Doak

The Old Course at St. Andrews includes several of the most renowned holes in the game. For me, though, there is one hole—often overlooked—that could serve as a model for golf course designers looking to counter the adverse effects of equipment technology: the Old Course's par-four, second hole. It rewards tactical play and the player who can control the trajectory of their approach shot, and it rewards imagination in the short game. On top of all that, it's unlike any other hole.

Like many of the outward holes at St. Andrews, the strategy of the second hole is profoundly simple: the more the hole is cut to the left side (or middle) of the double green, the more the tee-shot needs to be played to the fairway's right-hand side, close to the fairway bunkers and gorse along the boundary of the New Course. Every foot you play closer to the right yields a slightly better approach angle. If you don't drive the ball quite where you intended, it may be wise to adopt new tactics completely and play a defensive second shot—even from a good lie in the fairway.

The fairway is ample, but the second tee is jammed flush against the boundary, making it awkward to aim down the right-hand side. The wind tends to blow shots toward the middle of the course, so you can usually only hug the right-hand side by hitting a controlled left-to-right tee-shot back toward the 'danger' zone. At the same time, Cottage bunker, and the corner of the wall on the seventeenth hole, prevent long-hitters from merely bailing out to the left when driving.

The key feature of the hole is the unique contours at the front, left of the green, where a series of sharp ridges lie in front of the left-hand flagstick locations. If a high approach shot lands among these ridges, there is no telling where the ball might carom. The masterstroke is not to fly the ball close to the hole, but to land well short of the green and let the ball release; if played with the proper pace the ball will roll up and over the guardian ridges as if they didn't exist. For players whose talent or imagination limits them to hitting high approaches, their cause can be bolstered by playing to the right from the tee; even so, the approach must still be directed safely to the right side of the green to avoid the possibility of a bad bounce.

The ridges in front of the green have remained a talking point, and a strategic relevancy, for the longest time. One hundred years ago, the best players of the day had to hit the equivalent of a three-wood short of the ridges, and roll their ball over them, while short-hitters were forced to play their second shots safely to the right. Today, the green is much more receptive to short-hitters' long approaches, yet it coerces better players to hit a low shot from close in, instead of the high pitch they would normally elect to play. The ridges are a much more discerning hazard than a frontal bunker, which would extract the greatest penalty for a ball that came up short of the green. Ingeniously, the ridges serve as a hazard for the good player without bothering the average player too much.

Upon such a landscape, and considering the St. Andrews wind, it is easy to misjudge the approach and have your ball finish short of the green. When this occurs, golfers face the perplexing prospect of putting or chipping over the ridges, to try to get close to the hole. These ridges are quite severe, and I still remember Herbert Warren Wind's classic description of them: they are so abrupt it is possible that you could stand up to your putt and not see a man lying between you and the hole. It is a shot best played close to the ground, calling for a different kind of touch than most courses now require.

To be sure, the second hole at St. Andrews is not marked by the sort of terrific hazard—Strath, Hell bunker, the Principal's Nose, or the Road—which makes its more famous siblings so memorable. It is a hole brought to life by simple things, namely, the firmness of the ground, and the rippling undulations of the Old Course. In short, it is the quintessential links golf hole, and the perfect antithesis of the more Americanised pitch over the Swilcan Burn at the opening hole.

Renaissance Golf Design, Inc.
Traverse City, Michigan, USA

'Dyke'
Par-4
MEN'S: 411 Yards
WOMEN'S: 375 Yards (Par-5)
DESIGNER: Unknown

The National Golf Club, Australia

Seventh hole: 'Old' Course Ross Perrett

In spite of being a young club—barely sixteen years old—The National Golf Club at Cape Schanck on the Mornington Peninsula already has a proud history. In a flurry of activity to mark the new millennium, two new links-style courses were under construction, along with a new clubhouse, to complement its so-called 'Old' Course, which opened for play in 1988. The National was carved out of coastal woodland set high above the cliffs of Cape Schanck, overlooking Gunnamatta surf beach in the National Park beyond.

Brilliantly routed through difficult terrain by Robert Trent Jones Jr. and his team, the course is loved by the members, yet often unfairly maligned by the broader golfing public brought up on the subtleties of the Melbourne sandbelt courses. In part, this could be due to some of the greens being considered a little quirky, where golfers must exercise their imagination when assessing heavily breaking putts. One must also come to terms with The National's exacting greenside contours, and at various times during the round, it may be unwise when approaching to aim directly for the green. This certainly takes a deal of getting used to: local knowledge never goes astray!

In the golf-course architecture industry—perhaps as a concession to marketing—one often hears the term 'signature holes' being bandied about. And when such language arises, the countdown begins to arguments and tiffs, regarding the relative merits of golf holes. Yet, The National's short par-three, seventh hole—abutting a National Park and played across a deep ravine to a small, cliff-side, island green—is virtually everyone's choice. From day one it has been a favourite among members and visitors, alike, and is one of the most photographed holes in Australia. In truth, this little jewel owes its very existence to chance: the hole was initially designed as the fourth hole—to be played in reverse in the original layout. A loop of holes comprising the second, through fourth holes, was reversed to reduce the earthworks required to build the third hole. Equally importantly, it was a way of capitalising on the stunning coastline view that one of the course shapers spotted from high in his bulldozer cabin. While luck played its role in the birth of the second hole, great credit should be accorded to the

designers and the developers for having the courage to reroute the course during the construction phase. Many in the industry would baulk at such activity.

Following the development of the two new courses, and a new clubhouse in 2002, the second hole was renumbered to be the seventh. The hole itself hasn't changed, but the consequences of its changed position in the round have been significant. When played as the second hole, it required a very accurate shot when barely warmed up. Sure, one could encounter a troublesome breeze at the first, but being lenient in fairway width, it hardly made your knees tremble! The second hole, though, was the golfer's first real confrontation where the wind had such a profound influence on your game and state of mind. Played as the seventh hole, however, a golfer's joints are well 'oiled,' and ample time has passed to acclimatise to the wind of the day. When it was the second hole, one drawback was the high likelihood of arriving at the tee to find a hold-up in play—not surprisingly, often at club championship time when members were extra vigilant. The necessity of teeing-up in front of waiting groups only increased the intimidation factor.

Measuring 139 metres from the black championship tee, golfers are faced with a tee-shot that is all carry—nothing but dense scrub in the ravine between you, and the green. Fear is the architect's great weapon here, brought about by a combination of a target that is over forty-five metres wide, plus only eight-to-fifteen metres deep in places, and surrounded by severe penalty. And, of course, there is the ever-present wind howling down the coastline. Played into the teeth of the prevailing south-westerly, it is not unknown for powerful golfers to hit a three-iron, or even bigger firepower. And, so, having the honour is not always wise! With the summer easterly helping, however, the hole can be reduced to a mere flick with a pitching-wedge. Club selection, allied to an accurate assessment of the strength of the wind, is crucial.

There are two alternatives to landing on the green: 'bailing' out to a large bunker situated at the back, right-hand side of the green; or playing toward the fairway even further to the right. When the fierce south-west wind is in operation, faith in one's game

Par-3
MEN'S: 139 Metres
WOMEN'S: 107 Metres
DESIGNER: Robert Trent Jones Jr. (1985)

and a solid constitution is required. The prospect of aiming well left of the green—out to sea and in the direction of native 'jungle'—in the hope the wind will bring the ball back to the green, is not everyone's idea of a relaxing, good time! No doubt, the black tee confers the best view of the coastline and the beaches beyond. From this tee, one finds the angle of the green is dished, with a gentle 'backboard' that rewards a longer shot. And with the ravine staring you in the face, long is far preferable than short! George Munn, the shaper, 'buried an elephant' in the front of the green, and this needs to be cleared to avert your ball getting a nasty kick forward, or being repelled backward off the green. Aside from the middle-left portion of the green, an alternative pin placement can be found many metres away, well to the right, and short of the bunker on a narrow extension of the green. When the flagstick is positioned in this tight slither of land, the tee-shot is shorter—perhaps by a full club—than when the pin is located in the main body of the green, and it calls for precision play of the highest calibre.

From the blue tee, the hole is significantly shorter at 121 metres, and most players find it is less intimidating. The direction of play becomes more out to sea, and depending on the pin position of the day, this orientation often takes the existing backboard out of play. And as the hole is usually played with a more lofted club from the blue tee, the effect of the wind is exaggerated.

The Women's tee, with the green 107 metres distant, is cleverly positioned. It is located almost at right angles to the Men's tee, allowing the green to silhouette against the ocean beyond. A generous fairway lies in front of the green, but the opening to the green is narrow with the bunker more in play. From this tee, one mustn't go left, or be long.

Golf at its best, is a game in harmony with nature—a proposition that is evident in abundance at The National. The setting for the seventh hole is exceptional: a borrowed landscape of massive scale with long, distant views; and the ever-present noise of the sea below. The indigenous vegetation has been respected and this enhances a heroic hole that takes advantage of the natural terrain. Great holes abound everywhere, but the seventh hole will always be a favourite.

Thomson Perrett Pty Ltd
Melbourne, Victoria, Australia

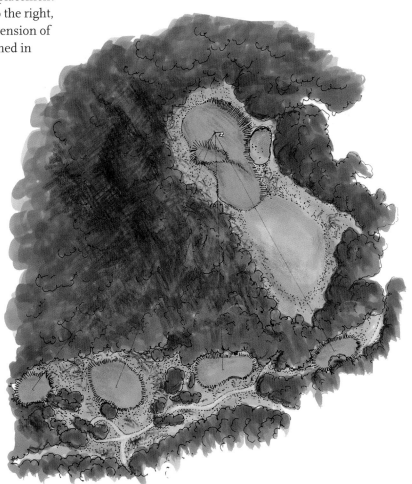

The National Golf Club (Old): Seventh hole, Australia.
(Photo by David Scaletti.)

Machrihanish Golf Club, Scotland
First hole Peter Fjallman

I t is known that golf was played at Machrihanish on Scotland's West Coast in the early 1870s. In 1876 a golf club known as the Kintyre Golf Club was formed, and it incorporated a ten-hole course laid out by the members along the linksland of Machrihanish Bay.

The club's professional, Charles Hunter, made some early alterations in the first year, extending the course to a twelve-hole layout. In 1879, reflecting its growing maturity and ambition, the club called upon the services of Old Tom Morris to assess the existing design and discuss the possibility of creating an eighteen-hole golf course.

The south-west tip of the Kintyre Peninsula is known for its beauty and remoteness, one can only imagine the arduous journey that Old Tom endured from St. Andrews. To reach Machrihanish he travelled by train, steamboat, and a long carriage drive. But he apparently found the trip worthwhile: his four-day stay was considerably longer than usual. The first time Old Tom laid eyes on Machrihanish, it is believed he said: 'Eh Mon! The Almichty had Gowf in his e'e when he made this place!'

Old Tom put forward three major suggestions: the acquisition of additional land; the creation of an eighteen-hole course; and most famously, the relocation of the first-tee position.

The first hole at Machrihanish confers one of the most spectacular views of any opening hole in golf. The proximity to the Atlantic Ocean, and the view of the hills of Kintyre, knit marvellously well to make the tee-shot the spectacle it is. We can assume that Old Tom had this in mind when he relocated the tee, but local legend has it that another circumstance was allocated more weight. According to club records, he wanted the first tee to be closer to the Pans Inn, where golfers were offered a taste of the local brew prior to teeing off.

In 1914—some thirty-five years after Old Tom's visit—English professional, J. H. Taylor, made improvements to the course, and the most recent major changes at Machrihanish took place after World War II by Sir Guy Campbell. Notwithstanding, Old Tom is owed a special thought of appreciation for providing us with not only one of the best opening holes, but surely one of the most exciting holes to be found anywhere.

In *The Spirit of St. Andrews* (1995), Alister Mackenzie defines an ideal golf hole. He states: 'The ideal hole is one that affords the greatest pleasure to the greatest number, gives the fullest advantage for accurate play, stimulates players to improve their game, and which never becomes monotonous.' In my opinion, the opening hole at Machrihanish—a par-four named 'Battery'—fulfils every criterion in being considered an ideal hole.

The hole is 428 yards from the back-tee, and it presents players with alternative routes for their tee-shot. The adventurous line is to cut the corner over the beach; when the tide is in, that entails taking on the Atlantic Ocean. A successful drive along this line rewards the player with an easier shot into the green with a mid-iron, effectively taking the front bunkers out of play. The conservative line is to aim for the middle of the fairway, thereby avoiding the beach and four bunkers on the fairway's right-hand side. Successfully achieved, your ball encounters a slope that exerts quite an influence on the ball's resting place, and your second-shot stance. After splitting the fairway, the next shot calls usually for an accurate long-iron into the green. The safest driving-line is to play well away from the beach, and well short of the first bunker on the right-hand side. This route will present

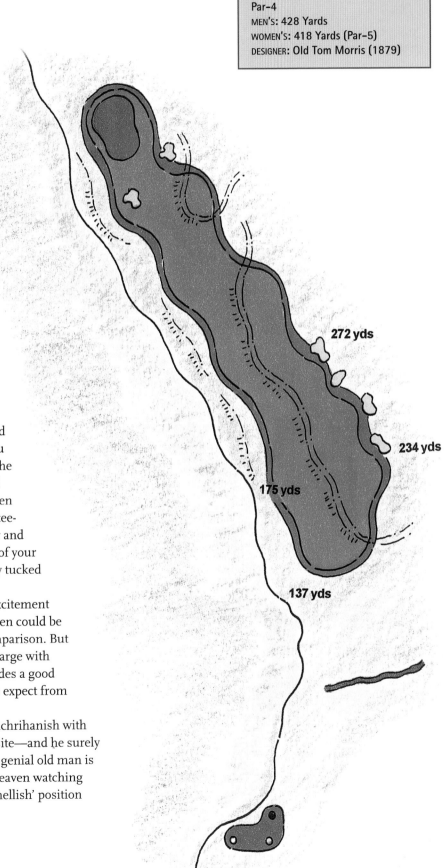

'Battery'
Par-4
MEN'S: 428 Yards
WOMEN'S: 418 Yards (Par-5)
DESIGNER: Old Tom Morris (1879)

the player with a very long second shot, and for most players the green will not be reachable. From this position of safety, however, the two bunkers in front of the green are now well in play. But there is another factor, over and above skill level, to consider when choosing which tee-shot route is appropriate.

The ever-changing weather in the area provides an extra dimension to the hole. When the Atlantic is showing its more fearful face with gusty winds, the alternatives from the tee are reduced. But on a calm and sunny day the tee-shot affords you plenty of options on how to play the hole, and there is always a special feeling looking across the bay when stepping onto the first tee. It is a tee-shot that is relived by golfers over and over; depending on the outcome of your tee-shot, a lesson should be safely tucked away for the next occasion.

With so much attention and excitement resting upon the tee-shot, the green could be viewed as a 'poor relation' by comparison. But it is an interesting feature itself: large with gentle rolling slopes, and it provides a good introduction to players of what to expect from the remaining greens.

Old Tom Morris compared Machrihanish with Paradise—there is also the opposite—and he surely knew if such a place existed. The genial old man is probably smiling in his golfing heaven watching the golfers hitting shots from a 'hellish' position on the beach.

Fjallman Golf Design
Åkersberga, Sweden

272 yds

234 yds

175 yds

137 yds

National Golf Links of America, USA

Seventeenth hole Scot Sherman

In my mind, the criteria for selection of a favourite golf hole begins with those associated with making a player think. And that's where the emphasis must lie. For such holes cannot fail to provide many playing options from the tee, requiring golfers to work the flight of their ball in multiple directions to gain the most advantage into the greens.

Although not a long hole, National's par-four, seventeenth hole demands all of the above, and it has been a much-admired and steadfast example of strategic golf. As the diagram clearly shows, this hole can be described as a S-shaped hole, providing the tactical twists and turns that give the players choices.

In horse racing, jockeys are known to 'ask the question' of their steed in the middle of a competition to see if it will 'answer,' meaning the rider will push their mount at the critical time in the hope that it will respond with the desire needed for victory. In the same way, golf architect Charles Blair Macdonald through his design asks the golfer to decide how they wish to attack this hole. The examination first takes place at the tee, which allows the player to respond in proportion to their desire and ability to produce a low score.

The simplest answer to conquer the seventeenth hole is to play a right-to-left shot along route-A, which provides the most direct line to the green, but this also requires the most precise stroke. If struck correctly, the shot will find its way over the diagonal expanse of hillocks, sand and tall grass on the left, and past central bunkers on the right to settle in the fairway short of the green. Depending on the amount of danger one wishes to face, the result could be a fairly straightforward and open approach. Furthermore, the best players can opt to play their tee-shot directly at the left side of the putting surface, seeking to avoid the hazards altogether. A mistake, however, can prove devastating as an overcooked attempt may find water, rough, or sand, to ruin visions of a potentially easy birdie.

The more timid answer to Macdonald's question is to play along route-B, which mostly avoids the perils of the aggressive tee-shot line. This route may suit the conservative player who prefers to make their move in the race a little further down the track. Those playing an approach from this position, however, are again faced with the stern question they declined to answer on the tee. The options are to play toward the narrow fairway short of the green, or go directly at the putting surface obscured by a prominent ridge. Golfers who insist upon going for the green must be precise, as a shot played too short will land in the ridge or bunkers, while a shot played too far will skip over the green into more sand or rough. Otherwise, a well-placed second shot to the left side should leave a chip-and-putt opportunity from in front of the green for a meandering par. Such are the options that fascinate every devout golfer.

The seventeenth hole, and the entire NGLA course for that matter, presents a beautiful setting in which to ponder the designer's many queries of our golf games. An additional feature of this great hole is the view from the elevated tee; by common consent it's the best on the course and it serves to distract the player from the task at hand. But that's okay: golf is meant to be a pleasure, never a chore! The Peconic Bay in the distance introduces another pleasing texture into the mottled landscape that golfers traverse during their round, while adding difficulty by altering depth perception. Although it is most appealing for a course to possess nuances that make us think, it doesn't hurt for the playing field to look good, too.

Golf architects are constantly on the lookout for interesting and exciting ways to challenge the players of today, and tomorrow. But we should never forget our roots. If nothing else, this favourite hole of mine teaches us that length, beauty, and notoriety, are secondary to the interest created by the choices we ask players to make.

Weed Design
Ponte Vedra Beach, Florida, USA

'Peconic'
Par-4
MEN'S: 375 Yards
WOMEN'S: 320 Yards
DESIGNER: Charles Blair Macdonald (1909)

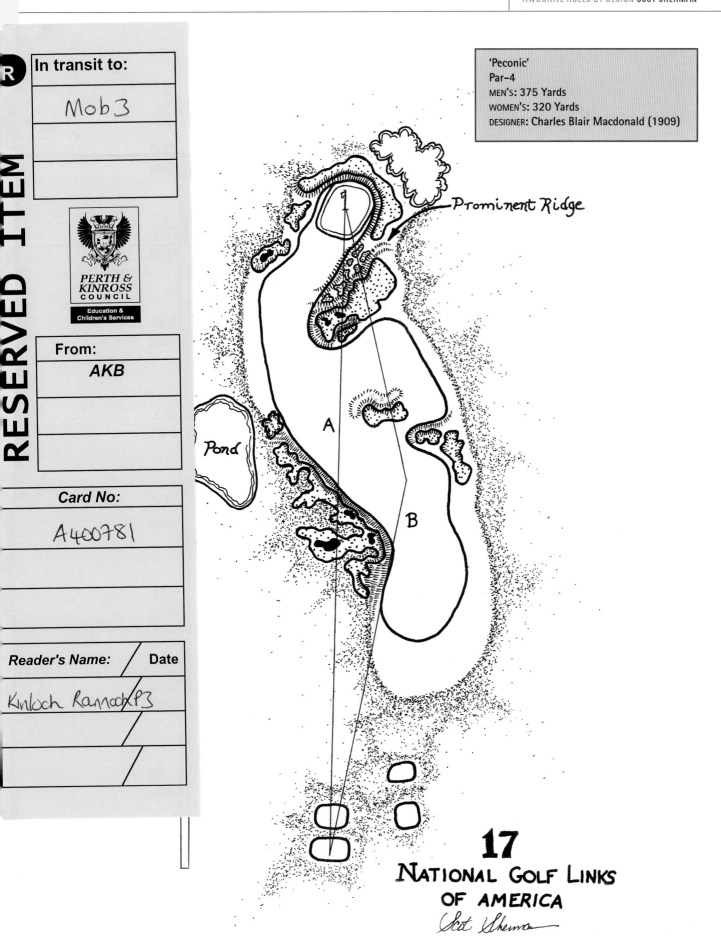

Prominent Ridge

Pond

A

B

17
NATIONAL GOLF LINKS
OF AMERICA

Scot Sherman

St. Andrews, Scotland

Seventeenth hole: Old Course Bob Harrison

During the last half of the twentieth century, golf commentators often argued over the merits of 'fairness' in golf-course design—something akin to a set of rules developed about fairness. Long par-fours, for example, were meant to have huge, uninteresting greens, and shallow fairway bunkers from which escape was mandatory. Such mental rigidity, however, has led to a situation where many of us are left to cringe at the sight of tournament players, particularly those in the USA, blithely hitting two-irons from little more than huge, flat, and uniformly groomed sand pits.

There is no unchallengeable set of rules on what constitutes a good golf hole! Moreover, we know that 'fair' does not always equate with 'good' and 'unfair' can sometimes be 'great.'

For the sake of the argument, let's just suppose that one of these commentators was the client for a proposed new golf course. Imagine their reaction following the golf architect's detailed explanation of one of the holes. Such an explanation may go as follows:

On one of the holes, toward the end of play, there will be Out of bounds on the right side and you can drive diagonally across it if you choose. The wind will often blow from left to right, and there will be a railway shed in front of the tee. This must be carried by golfers opting for the brave line, thereby, making the tee-shot 'blind.' We'll make the hole 461 yards and call it a par-four. We don't want to be complacent about the second shot, so to add some spice we'll build a shallow tabletop green set diagonally to the shot. Immediately behind the green there will be a railway line, where escape is very tricky indeed, and beyond the tracks a stonewall against which many a shot will come to rest. On the front, left of the green, there will be a pot-bunker—fiendishly deep—and even the front part of the green will disappear into it. Our team is also considering adding a one-to-two foot downslope in the green, away from the bunker, and toward the railway tracks. The hole might well catch on, but regardless, it promises to be a hole of some distinction. What do you think?

Would the client allow such a hole to be built? Surely the client's reaction would be one of being gob-smacked! But such a hole is already in existence, and it just so happens to be the most famous one in golf. And, arguably, among the best and the most difficult. Of course, it's the seventeenth hole at the Old Course, St. Andrews—the infamous Road hole. Granted, the railway track is now a paved road, and the railway sheds have been modernised and lost their charm, owing to a huge hotel development behind them. And three or four yards have been clipped, from what was originally a par-five. But this wonderful hole is still there after hundreds of years, and it remains as feared and strategically interesting as it was originally.

The sometimes-devastating effect that fitness programmes, along with the latest generation of equipment advances, have unleashed on the strategic merits of many courses is a hot topic these days. Even though the Road hole is no longer a par-five, and can often be reached with a mid- to short-iron, the interest level and respect from golfers has never waned.

It takes a brave and precise tee-shot across the sheds and along the 'blind' Out of bounds to enable the easiest approach from the fairway's right-hand side—particularly when there is a strong wind howling from left to right. The 'safer' drive to the left side of the fairway can easily run out of fairway, resulting in a longer approach with a bad angle to the green, and, sometimes, from a difficult lie in the rough. But if you do find yourself playing from the left, the smart approach is toward the green's front, right-hand side, or just short of the green. In this situation, a running-shot shaped ever so slightly (right to left) might even chase onto the putting surface. Following a long putt, or chip, up the slope onto the main plateau of the green, recording a par is quite possible. But it is also possible to get the angles wrong and finish with bogey, or worse, if the putt finishes in the Road bunker.

The case for risking the daring tee-shot line becomes evident upon reaching the green. And the second shot is arguably even more outrageous than the drive. At all costs you must avoid the Road bunker, from which escape is often so difficult. Then there is the raised, angled, and shallow green; the quick drop three to four feet down to the path; plus the road. All of

'Road'
Par-4
MEN'S: 461 Yards
WOMEN'S: 426 Yards (Par-5)
DESIGNER: Unknown

these features conspire to make the approach one of the most demanding in golf. And in most circumstances, the human element won't help much, either! If the pin is positioned to the left behind the Road bunker, it takes a very precise shot—probably working from right to left—to get really close. Discounting flukes, such a shot is really only feasible from the right side of the fairway after a long and daring drive.

Because of the angle of the green, managing both the length and direction of the approach is critical to your outcome. The right side of the green can be approached with a running shot, or one through the air. When the pin is tucked directly behind the bunker it can only be reached through the air. Such golfing bravado can only succeed with first-class execution, along with nerves of steel.

All of the difficulties and drama are heightened because the Road hole is the penultimate hole: sometimes of the Open Championship. Tournament players compiling a wonderful sub-par round know that their score is in total jeopardy until they pass the seventeenth hole.

Just ask Japanese professional, Tommy Nakajima. In the 1978 Open Championship, he was in contention standing on this tee on the third day and would have been relieved to reach the front of the green in two shots, albeit, with a tricky putt across the rolling section of the green. Nakajima was all at sea with the angles, and his ball disappeared into the Road bunker. Four shots later, he found the putting surface again and finished with a nine.

Or Tom Watson! Playing in the last group in the final round of the 1984 Open, Watson stood on the Road hole fairway locked in a titanic struggle with Seve Ballesteros, who was one hole ahead and about to sink a birdie putt on the home green. After some indecision, Watson selected a two-iron and pushed the shot just a little to the right, but it was too long. The back of the green is closer on this line, and so his ball scuttled over the green, the path and the road, finishing very close to the wall. In spite of having a restricted backswing, Watson managed to get the ball back onto the green. Two putts later: the Open and any chance of a record-equalling sixth victory had gone.

Of course, it is not just the awesome nature of the hole that makes it such a favourite: the setting is inspiring. The big, open expanse of the last few holes of the Home of Golf, in the shadow of the beautiful old town. A university town at that, with a philosophy department! I've often considered this to be the ideal place to sit around and think about the meaning of life. Then the famous links beckons for a brisk three-hour encounter, followed by three or four pints. Life and golf at St. Andrews: it doesn't get much better than this.

Greg Norman Golf Course Design
Sydney, NSW, Australia

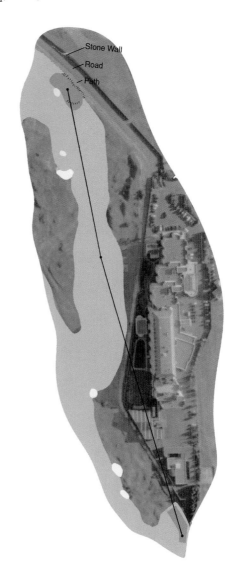

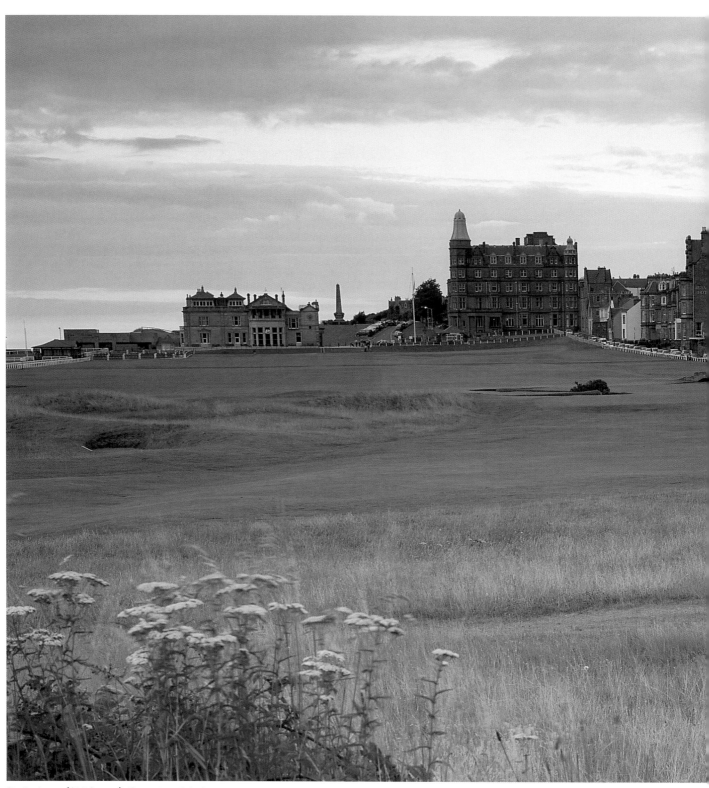

St. Andrews (Old Course): Seventeenth hole,
Scotland. (Photo by David Scaletti.)

Royal County Down Golf Club, Northern Ireland

Thirteenth hole Todd Eckenrode

My introduction to Royal County Down Golf Club while competing in the 1999 British Amateur Championship was a brutal experience. A couple of practice rounds under my belt only served to further open my eyes to the many terrors that exist over this incredibly rugged golfing terrain. Sometimes, you're better off not knowing! My feelings of trepidation during competition, however, were tempered with greater feelings of excitement, fascination, and wonder, as I continually explored the intricacies of this great golfing links.

Many of the holes require substantial carries over the intimidating, massive dunes to landing areas that are blind to the golfer. This precedent continues throughout the course of your round, and a general feeling of uneasiness permeates, as the final destination of your shot is frequently unknown. It is vital to focus on a target, to trust your instincts of orientation, and, most importantly, to trust your swing. It is these qualities in play that make the long par-four, thirteenth at Royal County Down my favourite hole.

Interestingly, the tee-shot on the thirteenth differs from many others at Royal County Down in that the landing area is relatively visible ahead of you, with the fairway nestled into a valley between two dunal ridges. When I played the famous old links, the dunes on the left-hand side were covered in gorse, virtually ensuring that a ball hit to the left was lost. However, the dunes on the right were considerably more open and varied in vegetation. Clumps of gorse were scattered about, but predominately, the tall natural grasses covered this lower lying ridge immediately adjacent to the fairway. During the Amateur, the length of the hole mandated a driver off the tee for most players; if the hole happened to be downwind, or if you were a long hitter, then a safer club selection could be utilised.

The key to the hole, though, is how the right-hand side dunes affect the golfer's approach shot. After the landing area—approximately 100 yards short of the green—a ridge encroaches completely into the centreline of the shot, obscuring visibility to the entire green. The pin, however, can usually be seen fluttering in the wind. Depending on your position in the fairway, you may also catch a glimpse of the left-hand greenside bunker, which provides a minor gauge on the green's proximity and distance.

This encroaching ridge is scattered with a variety of nasty bunkers, tall grass clumps, and thick gorse. In essence: it couldn't be much more intimidating. And though its effects cross back out of the centreline to continue up the far right side of the green, the ridge appears to continue right up to the green itself. In reality, the approach into the green is quite open, and it encourages a running shot to scurry on up to the pin. And yet, your instincts tell you that may be the last shot in the world to play! This contradiction is just one of several factors that makes the hole so interesting, forcing you to trust what you know to be factual, and not what your eyes might be relaying back.

To further heighten the effect, the bunkering set into this ridge is characteristic of the wonderfully unique style throughout Royal County Down. How I love this trademark rugged natural style of bunker, with its dark imposing lips that can be quite thick in spots and accented with tufts of tall natural grasses of contrasting colours along the top. The visual effect is that of a colossal bunker—vertically immense—where escape seems ever so difficult.

All of us have a tendency to play toward what we can see. Ultimately, this is a more comfortable feeling than flying blind, and it lures the golfer to play toward the left side of the thirteenth green. But this is a dangerous play, and precisely where the lone bunker adjacent to the green is situated—a brilliantly placed hazard that infiltrates the golfer's psyche, if ever one did. The greatest holes in the world are those in which the golfer is challenged both physically and mentally, and the thirteenth at Royal County Down certainly meets that criteria.

Todd Eckenrode–Origins Golf Design
Irvine, California, USA

Par-4
MEN'S: 443 Yards
WOMEN'S: 406 Yards
DESIGNER: George Combe (1903)

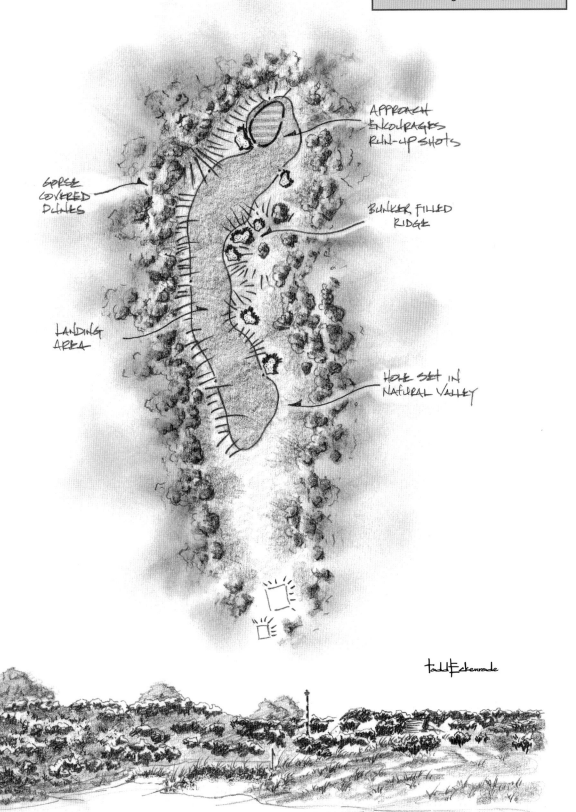

APPROACH
ENCOURAGES
RUN-UP SHOTS

GORSE
COVERED
DUNES

BUNKER FILLED
RIDGE

LANDING
AREA

HOLE SET IN
NATURAL VALLEY

Todd Eckenrode

Spyglass Hill Golf Course, USA

Fourth hole Donald Knott

What a special hole the par-four, fourth at Spyglass Hill is: one of the truly great holes in the world of golf. This medium-length hole of 379 yards from the back-tee showcases the very essence of the game, blending seamlessly and artistically into a magnificent natural landscape. All elements of golfing values, and landscape, harmonise in perfect balance, which results in an unmatched golf experience.

The hole has abundant beauty, significant intimidation, and a bit of mystery, for players of varying golfing skill. As far as designs go, this is Robert Trent Jones in full stride, circa 1966.

Slightly doglegging to the left and terraced into the dunes, a golfer's gaze is directed naturally to the green: over the dune landscape to a flag peaking its head out from a narrow dune valley, some thirty feet below the level of the tee. Another pleasing aspect to the eye: the fairway tilts gently from right to left, and creates a comfortable fit for an ideal shot of similar shape. The landforms and vegetation further enhance the flow of the hole. A tall stand of dark-green pines frames the high, right-hand side of the hole. The lower, left-hand side of the fourth features a rolling, light-coloured dunescape, which further accentuates the comfortable right-to-left movement of the hole. However, no amount of spectacular beauty is able to camouflage its terrifying difficulty.

The narrow, ribbon-like green slides naturally downhill in a narrow valley between steep dunes. Negotiation of the green's intricacies is the cornerstone of Spyglass's fourth's greatness. The green is downright skinny: only five yards wide at the front, and about ten yards in width at the lower rear portion.

Any ball that fails to find the green and finds the dunes instead will, most likely, result in an unplayable lie for the golfer. Ice plant, a thick, succulent groundcover, forms the basis of the havoc that follows any wayward approach. This hole could easily be benchmarked: a classic example of the relationship between maintenance characteristics, and difficulty. The extent and thickness of the Ice plant—occasionally purged—has a direct effect on the hole's playability. This tiny strip of a green is such a demanding and intimidating target, that golfers are forced to make a wise, yet difficult, decision on the tee. Gaining the shortest possible approach to the green is clearly advantageous: the longer tee-shot confers a significant advantage to those looking for one. However, a longer tee-shot can only be attempted at considerable risk to one's score. The fairway narrows significantly for long-ball hitters, setting up the textbook risk-and-reward option from the tee. Other than a bone-crunching drive, which leaves the player a short pitch from an ideal angle, one obvious tee-shot option is the use of a long-iron. And, assuming the fairway is then safely found, this generally leaves a highly taxing mid-iron to the miniscule green. The brave tee-shot option is too tempting for many to handle sensibly, where a slight error may result in an unplayable lie, or a lost ball.

A tee-shot of 290 yards, to an eighteen-yard wide landing area (A) will leave a pitch of seventy to one hundred yards, down the long axis of the fifty-five-yard deep green. A comfortable 220-yard drive (from the back tee) to a forty-five-yard wide fairway (B) will leave a 140 to 170-yard semi-blind, angled approach over ice plant-covered dunes—intimidating to say the least. By playing short, and right, one may avoid the dunes, but the chances are you'll be greeted by an awkward lie in the rough, or face a shot from the bunker perched above the green. The bottom line: a clear head; knowledge of one's playing ability; and two well-executed shots. Nothing less is required to find the green!

Finding the green in regulation figures is a spectacular feat, but work remains to be done as the fourth green falls some six feet from front to back. The green's front portion—some forty-five feet—is narrow, and falls steeply away from the shot, to a deck area fifty-feet long and some twenty-three feet in width. Beyond this deck, the green rolls to a lower level of soft undulation, gradually falling toward the ocean. Although slightly larger—some seventy feet in length and thirty feet in width—this lower level is surrounded by dunes and a small pot-bunker.

Executing two perfect shots in clam conditions is no easy task, but a quantum leap in difficulty awaits golfers when playing this hole into the prevailing afternoon breeze, or the more significant winter winds. Because the hole is only modest in length, golfers of varying abilities have essentially similar options, and face similar dilemmas. The beauty of these shorter holes is that all golfers can dream of executing two perfect shots, then converting with a single putt. If that dream comes true at 'Blind Pew,' it will be a memory to last a lifetime.

As a golf hole, the fourth at Spyglass Hill has it all: a magnificent setting along the sea and in the dunes; and a striking example of golf-course architecture that created an experience rarely equalled in the world of golf.

Knott Brooks Linn Golf Course Design Group
Mountain View, California, USA

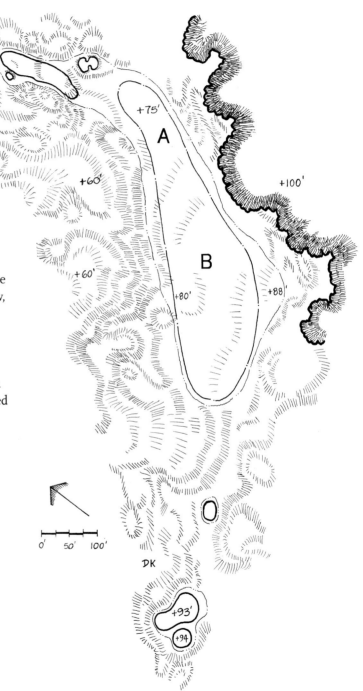

'Blind Pew'
Par–4
MEN'S: 379 Yards
WOMEN'S: 299 Yards
DESIGNER: Robert Trent Jones Sr. (1966)

Durban Country Club, South Africa
Second hole Phil Jacobs

The Durban Country Club in South Africa and its layout is steeped in history and tradition, having hosted many professional golf tournaments, including fifteen South African Opens since 1924. One section of the golf course is located on old dune type terrain—the course is only about 100 metres from the sea—while the balance is located on what used to be marshy areas, close to the estuary of a major river. The first three holes generally play into the prevailing wind and under such conditions can be extremely daunting to all but the finest players. According to some judges, the opening five holes represent the best opening holes in golf.

The focus of my essay is the second hole: a truly spectacular par-three. On a typically windy Durban day, the elevated tee-shot makes for an intimidating scene, with golfers fully exposed to the elements. And when playing from elevated tees, most golfers do find it a struggle to 'knock' the ball down. Under windy conditions, recording a par on this wonderful hole is satisfying for all levels of golfers. However, on a calm day, golfers in a relaxed state can readily appreciate the setting and the undoubted beauty of the hole, without being overawed by it.

While the majority of the green's surface is relatively flat, the front of the green features a steep slope toward the tee, ensuring that balls pitching toward the front portion of the green usually feed down to a valley some metres short of the green.

Should a tee-shot be struck only marginally left, or right, of the target it will find a bunker, while a slashing cut or a hooked shot is destined to find the bushes. Durban Country Club aside, many architects and clubs aim to ease golfers into their rounds by way of lenient or 'soft' first and second holes. Where this has occurred, players are spared the 'intimidation' factor; the fact that most golfers won't be fully warmed-up, or settled into their round, becomes less of an issue than it does at Durban Country Club.

Teeing off in the fourth round of the 1973 South African Open, Alan Henning was in contention to win the tournament. During the last round of play, however, competitors were dogged by crosswinds and, at the second hole, Henning ended up hitting the ball way to the left, off the green and down an embankment. With his ball coming to rest approximately twelve metres below the level of the green's surface, one can imagine the head scratching that took place as he weighed up his options. Sparing you all the sordid details, Henning ended up making a quadruple-bogey seven, which virtually snuffed out his round and tilt at the title. Bob Charles, the reliable and accurate New Zealander professional took top honours on this day.

Phil Jacobs Golf Course Designer
George, South Africa

Par-3
MEN'S: 172 Metres
WOMEN'S: 140 Metres
DESIGNER: Laurie Waters (1923)

Koninklijke Haagsche Golf & Country Club, The Netherlands

Sixth hole Kyle Phillips

The Royal Haagsche was designed by Harry Shapland Colt in 1926. Having designed courses in Europe for nearly twenty years, I have found only a few people who are genuinely knowledgeable about the great links and heathland courses of The Netherlands. If not for being commissioned by the club to assist them with several restoration issues, I, too, might have missed this grand old links.

Situated on one of the most magnificent golfing dunescapes, this Colt gem is one of the best-kept secrets of links golf. Colt was summoned to the site by the owner, a munitions mogul, who wanted to construct his own private golfing playground. Ironically, the impetus for the project revolved around him being barred access to the original Koninklijke Haagsche Golf & Country Club course, which was then located in the flat land nearer to Den Haag. Although Colt had designed courses on some of the most incredible canvases, even he must have been astonished when first casting his eyes on this expansive area of linksland. When designing the course, he left the original dunes virtually untouched, allowing the fairways to follow the dramatically undulating terrain.

My favourite hole on the course is the sixth hole, a 420-yard par-four. As a left-to-right dogleg hole, it plays to a slightly elevated green that falls away on all sides, with only a sliver of dune supporting a back right-hand side pin.

The safe drive is down the centre of the fairway, leaving approximately 180 yards into the green. It is, however, the difficulty of the green, which is more receptive to a shorter iron that forces players to seriously consider making the diagonal carry over the natural dunescape from the tee. If one does not perfectly execute a drive that combines proper distance and direction, one will be playing one's second from either the blind natural crevasse that guards the inside of the carry, or the equally difficult large dune that snares balls through the fairway.

The slightly detached front-left greenside bunker—the sixth hole's lone bunker—is barely visible from limited vantage points. Along with the cascading edges of the putting surface, they combine to create a great sucking sound that can be heard when standing over one's approach shot. All it takes is a little pull of the hands or the slightest movement of the ball at the mercy of the prevailing breezes, and one's ball will be gobbled up by the bunker. From this position one is sure to remember Thomas Bjorn, who lost the 2003 Open Championship at Royal St. George's when his ball twice found its way back into the bunker after coming up just a few feet short of the pin.

At times it may be prudent to 'bail' out to the right, however, that option will result in your third shot being played from a deep and tightly mown swale. When the favoured club pin position is on the right, golf shots can easily be misjudged and pull up short, returning to the hollow from where they came. But when the pin is stationed to the left, one must take care not to pitch past the pin, as the closely shaven slope beyond will draw the ball into the left, greenside bunker.

With this little recognised design, Colt has once again displayed his masterful routing abilities by utilising the natural dunes and contours at just the right angles. In the process, the old master created a golf hole as strategic and thrilling as you will find anywhere in the world.

Kyle Phillips Golf Course Design
Granite Bay, California, USA

Note: 'Koninklijke' translates to 'Royal' in the English language.

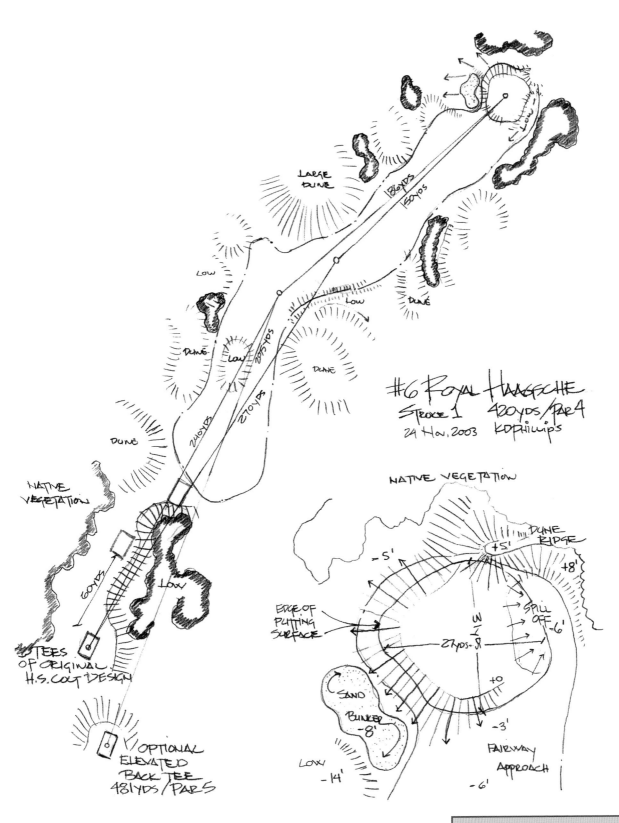

#6 Royal Haagsche
Stroke 1   420 yds / Par 4
24 Nov. 2003   KDPhillips

186 yds
150 yds

LARGE DUNE

LOW

LOW

DUNE

LOW

DUNE

LOW

DUNE

205 yds

240 yds

270 yds

DUNE

NATIVE VEGETATION

60 yds

LOW

3 TEES OF ORIGINAL H.S. COLT DESIGN

OPTIONAL ELEVATED BACK TEE 481 YDS / PAR 5

NATIVE VEGETATION

+5'   DUNE RIDGE

-5'   +8'

SPILL OFF -6'

EDGE OF PUTTING SURFACE

27 yds

+0

SAND BUNKER -8'

-3'

LOW -14'

FAIRWAY APPROACH

-6'

Par-4
MEN'S: 440 Metres
WOMEN'S: 334 Metres (Par-5)
DESIGNER: Harry S. Colt (1926)

The Royal Melbourne Golf Club, Australia
Third hole: West Course Harley Kruse

In an ongoing pursuit of studying golf holes and the game's art and literature, one becomes acquainted with the so-called 'best' holes, which, of course, are not necessarily destined to be classified as 'favourite' holes. For me, the latter group is as much defined by emotion as it is by the objective merits of a hole, and its architecture. This is the story about my favourite: the third hole on Royal Melbourne's West Course.

As a young Landscape Architecture graduate already working for a golf-course design firm in my hometown of Melbourne, I was taken by surprise to learn that that my long-deceased, Welsh-born grandfather had—apart from being an agronomist—served time as a 'Keeper of the Green.' Some may call my discovery destiny, while others would dismiss it as purely being in the genes. J. Leslie Rees was an agronomist in the truest sense of the word, and during World War II he not only researched and bred improved pasture grasses, but he tendered a nine-hole links at Skegness in Lincolnshire, UK. Upon returning to Australia, he wrote a book called *Lawns, Greens, and Playing Fields* (1962). By the time I finally reached up to grab the dusty volume off the bookshelf—to actually read it for the first time—it was another welcome surprise to discover that it contained a small chapter on golf-course design.

Around about the same period, it was the occasion of a new book celebrating one man's life's work in turf. I had the distinct pleasure of meeting its author, a gentleman named Claude Crockford. For many, he remains Australia's greatest ever 'Keeper of the Green'. Claude's nurturing and stewardship of Royal Melbourne—for the better part of forty years—saw his two courses regarded among the finest in the world. His preparation of the Composite Course for the 1959 Canada Cup put this layout on the championship golfing map. He did it again for the 1972 tournament, by then it was known as The World Cup. Claude's influence on future generations of turf managers perpetuates to this day. The photos intended for his book, *The Complete Golf Course: Turf and Design* (1993), were taken with his old Brownie camera, perhaps a decade or so earlier. For one reason or another, they didn't quite make the grade, so I had the fortunate task of reshooting many pictures. Part of my brief included capturing a section of Royal Melbourne's third on the West Course.

From the Men's tee, the third is a truly classic short par-four of only 324 metres. As the entrée to undoubtedly one of the greatest sequences of holes in golf—the fourth through sixth—it appears to be a fairly straightforward hole from the tee. This hole, however, sparkles with subtlety and brilliance. Flanked by tea-tree on both sides of the fairway, the hole doglegs to the left, while a large Cypress tree on the inside corner dissuades many golfing 'brutes' from the prospect of driving the green. And, yet, I was privileged to witness Tiger Woods achieve the feat in a practice round at the 1998 Presidents Cup. Before a caddie in the previous group had the chance to put the flagstick back into the cup, Tiger's ball had flown the Cypress and landed in front of the green. It bounced and rolled toward the cup, momentarily striking the back lip, before rolling on. The small crowd clapped in awe, and then he two-putted for the easiest birdie imaginable.

For most golfers, the third hole is best played with a three-metal, or long-iron, from the slightly elevated tee. Hitting over a typical Royal Melbourne carry—sandbelt heath and wild grasses—to the couch fairway, gently rising to the landing area, the tee-shot is often best placed left of the fairway's middle when the pin is stationed well to the right, and, conversely, to the fairway's far right in the advent of a left-hand-side pin position. Two fairway bunkers short, right on the fairway, are merely visual and curiosity features these days. The key when driving is to

Par-4
MEN'S: 324 Metres
WOMEN'S: 285 Metres
DESIGNER: Alister Mackenzie (1926)

not hit the ball too far on the straight line. Balls can easily wind up in the far rough, from where the angle to the green will be poor.

Getting to the nub of this great hole, it is with the short, fiendish second shot, and the 'all-world' green, where this hole becomes really interesting—most players are happy to walk off with a par on their card. This especially applies at tournament time when Royal Melbourne's greens are famously firm and fast. When approaching the green, players must figure out how to best deal with a deep, long, and diagonal hollow in front of the green. It gathers-up and slews weak shots to the right—toward the small, deep greenside bunker. Two bunkers lurk alongside the left of the green, but the key to the short game on the third hole is landing the ball precisely—not quite on a dime, but not far off it—on account of the green sloping heavily from front to back. This distance-control factor is critical. Perhaps seeing more greens being designed in this manner—with Royal Melbourne's third hole as the model—is something contemporary golf-course architects could consider emulating more often. For when the pin is located at the front of the green, I've watched even the best professionals come unstuck. When the approach is pitched too far, one has to expect a huge putt back up the slope. For those who get too 'cute' with their approach, there is every chance that they'll be blasting out of the sand on their third shot, or perhaps 'fiddling' around in the front swale.

While working on Claude's book, I headed down to Black Rock to catch the late-afternoon light. At this time, I had only played the West Course once, and when strolling across the first fairway I was surprised to discover there was no one around the opening holes. Arriving at the third green, it became apparent that I had this wonderful place all to myself. It was such an uplifting feeling. With plenty of time to set up and catch the preferred sun angle, I was able to see first-hand what Claude had been taking about a few days earlier. Being a close associate of Mick Morcom—and a few years later in 1935 appointed his assistant—he had witnessed the construction of much of the two courses, and this included the third green on the

West Course, and its surrounds. Claude fondly recalled the machinery of the day as being 'horse and scoop,' along with 'good ol shovels and man-power' for the fine work. In front of the third green, tightly mown fairway mounds were like waves, and troughs, in the sea. All these years later, the result of the hand of man—and horse—working closely with nature, had remained a truly wonderful sight. I tried my best to capture this with my camera, the sun now positioned low, and the light warm. And it was at this precise moment that it finally dawned upon me just what a wonderful profession golf-course architecture could be. From then on, this would be my chosen path, and the third on Royal Melbourne's West Course would always remain my favourite hole.

Greg Norman Golf Course Design
Sydney, New South Wales,
Australia

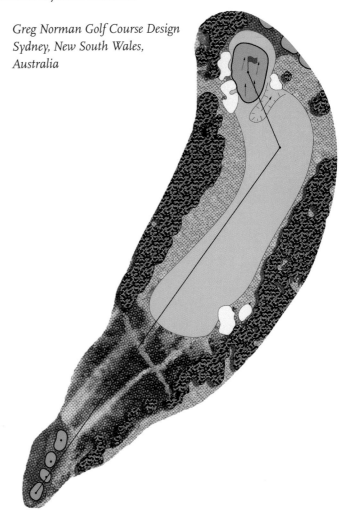

Lahinch Golf Club, Ireland
Fifth hole Brett Mogg

In his 1897 reworking of Lahinch, Old Tom Morris created two unique holes: the par-three, sixth hole known as Dell; and the fifth hole, Klondyke. Both have stood the rigorous test of time, and are as engaging and fun to play today, as they reportedly were in the glorious days of the gutty and hickory-shafted clubs. More recently, under the direction of consultant architect, Martin Hawtree, Lahinch has been redesigned. The Dell hole is now played as the fifth, while Klondyke is the fourth hole.

When famed architect Dr Alister Mackenzie first arrived at Lahinch in 1928 to undertake a remodelling of the existing links, the temptation to eliminate these holes must have been strong. Although his thoughts on these two holes are unrecorded, it is fairly obvious that they do not possess many of the characteristics typically found in a Mackenzie hole. Perhaps just enough Irish blood coursed through his veins to allow him to see the humour and joy inherent in these unconventional 'lay of the land' designs.

Blind holes are generally an anathema to almost all golf architects today, mainly for reasons of safety—read liability—but also for so-called 'fairness'—a style of thinking that permeates not only golf but also society at large. Aesthetics also are important in today's marketing-driven world: that which cannot be seen cannot be beautiful; and that which is not beautiful does not photograph well; and that which does not photograph well does not sell!

For the Dell hole—a creation as much of nature, as of humans—such considerations are of no consequence, for this is raw golf at its truest, where notions of fairness, aesthetics and beauty have no part in the golfing equation. With Dell, there is just the land, the wind, the golfer, the ball, and the hole—surely the very essence of the game.

At only 155 yards, there does not seem much about the Dell hole to inspire or intimidate golfers. In fact, it would be hard to imagine any golfer being intimidated by this hole, lacking as it is in both yardage and hazards. The landform is pedestrian and dead flat for the first 135 or so yards, before rising precipitously over the last twenty yards.

The wind factor aside, Dell's main defences consist of steep sand dunes—fronting and backing—covered in deep, fescue roughs. Combined with a long, narrow green—only a few paces deep in places—regulars to Lahinch know only too well that being one step long, or short, of the green will result in the golfer having an exacting 'up-and-down' for par: one of the most difficult imaginable. This knowledge is enough to create doubts in the minds of many golfers, and doubts are all that are required to turn a pure swing into one that collapses and produces a false shot.

For low-handicap golfers, snaring a birdie-two is a tantalising prospect—almost as close to a 'sure' thing as one can appear to be. So, when disaster strikes—and it surely will if you play the hole enough times—it can be a real body blow, coming as it does on such a seemingly easy hole. Part of Dell's appeal is that it has remained eminently playable for the young, the old, or the incompetent. The reason is simple: any thinned, tee-shot along the ground to the right, away from the flag, can still find an opening to the green, where there is every chance of scrambling a par.

Above all, the Dell's most endearing quality is its habit of turning adult golfers into children. There is something truly childlike and innocent in the joy of hitting a purely struck short-iron over the white rock on your chosen line; feeling your ball is close, knowing in your heart it's close, and then almost skipping all the way to the green to discover your fate. On account of its raw naturalness, plus an uncanny inclination to bring out the child in even the dourest of golfers, the Dell remains my favourite golf hole.

Nelson & Haworth
Golf Course Architects
Singapore

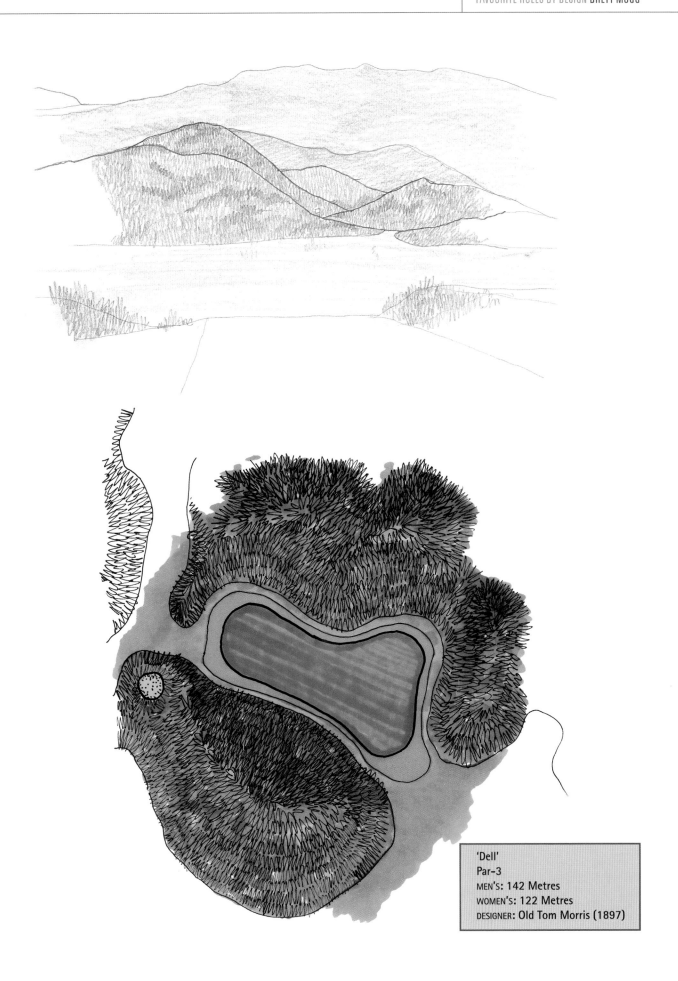

'Dell'
Par-3
MEN'S: 142 Metres
WOMEN'S: 122 Metres
DESIGNER: Old Tom Morris (1897)

Shinnecock Hills Golf Course, USA
Twelfth hole Simon Gidman

One of my early memories of college is that of the lecturer in historic landscapes repeatedly referring to gardens as palimpsests, knowing full well that us first-year students had no idea what he was talking about. Of course, after the lecture, we all scuttled off to the nearest dictionary to find the following explanation: a manuscript in which old writing has been rubbed out to make room for new. If the description of a palimpsest can be directed at a garden landscape, it can certainly be applied to a golf course.

So many of our great golf courses have undergone transformations over the years. Courses with often fairly inauspicious beginnings have been improved to become testaments to great golf-course architecture. Situated on the eastern seaboard of America, Shinnecock Hills Golf Club is certainly one of those courses.

Initially, Shinnecock was a reservation for the Alonquin tribe who roamed from Shinnecock Bay to Montauk. The symbol of the American Red Indian is entwined into all aspects of the club, most notably on the club's motif.

Designed in 1891 by Willie Davis, the golf course was initially a twelve-hole layout. Being a forerunner and early adopter of golf in America, so much happened at Shinnecock Hills. It was constantly introducing new ideas and forever moving forward. It was not the first course laid-out in America, but the first—possibly along with Chicago golf course—to have eighteen holes. It was the first to have a clubhouse, the first to be an incorporated golf club, and was possibly the originator of the use of the colour red for the Women's tees, when an additional nine holes—the Red Course—was designed for the exclusive use of the lady players. This separate Red Course was not an overwhelming success. Soon after opening, the two courses were rearranged to form a single eighteen-hole layout.

As great as these changes and innovations were, perhaps the biggest changes to the golf course came in 1928. It was in this landmark year that club president Mr. Lucien Tyng, purchased new land for development, and, subsequently, employed golf architect Dick Wilson. His constructors, Toomey and Flynn, were also brought into the fold to reorganise the layout. This work was completed in 1931 and it is broadly this layout that forms the basis of the golf course today. The changes undertaken increased the length of the course from less than 5,000 yards, to 6,749 yards. Between the early 1930s, and when the course was used for the 1986 US Open, another 163 yards were added to create the current 6,912-yard layout that plays to a stern par of seventy.

There are so many great holes at Shinnecock Hills, and normally you find that the thirteenth and fourteenth are the ones that seem to receive the most plaudits. However, to my way of thinking, the par-four, twelfth hole is the one that typifies its great architecture. Perhaps this is because it comes after the slightly disappointing short par-three, eleventh hole, or perhaps it was because I took a double-bogey five on the eleventh, yet parred the twelfth hole. I don't know.

But after a short walk uphill from the eleventh green, you cannot help but be immediately impressed by the shape, scale and arrangement of the twelfth hole. Being a reasonably straight hole played in its own amphitheatre, the hole measures 472 yards and plays over undulating terrain. There is no unforeseen trickery about the hole—what you see is what you get! The architects have not needed to overcomplicate, or exaggerate, the design. The hole is set in its own vast expanse, with no other golf hole in sight, and somehow this makes the dual between the player, and the game, even more intense and personal. The twelfth at Shinnecock is a marvellously thought out, and beautifully presented hole. The choices off the tee are almost unlimited. The easy drive is to the left of the central fairway bunker, where the bulk of the rolling fairway is, until a distant fairway bunker beckons at around 250 yards. The better golfer will either take on the central or right-hand bunkers to gain as much length as possible and reduce the pressure on the long, second shot.

The approach to the green is protected by a series of bunkers—almost penal in nature—with sand either side of the fairway. Yet for those who have taken the easy option from the tee, and played to the left of the fairway, the second shot is a serious challenge. When a decision has been made that the green is out of reach,

Par-4
MEN'S: 469 Yards
WOMEN'S: 427 Yards
DESIGNER: Dick Wilson (1928–31)

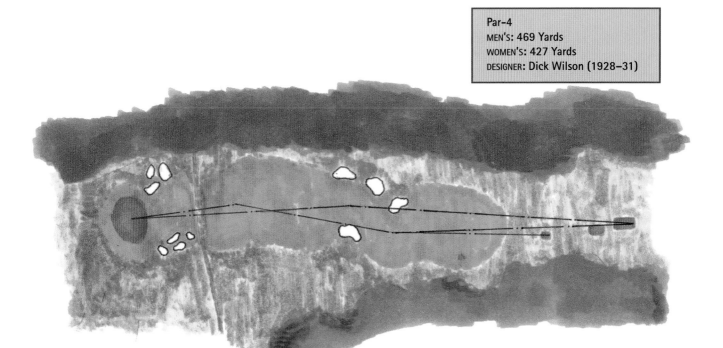

the golfer is left to decide upon the best second-shot strategy: a right-to-left shot into the very narrow space that is the approach; or to play short of the road, and chip from there. For those who have braved the narrow right-hand side of the fairway—avoiding bunkering at the 250-yard mark—the approach shot is, while shorter, equally challenging. The green tends to shed the ball into a series of hollows and swales off the putting surface. In order to hit an accurate shot to it, it's critical to your cause not to wind up in the fairway bunkering. There is no let up on the hole; the decision made on the tee needs to be carefully considered, the drive properly and powerfully struck, while the second shot demands clear thinking and accuracy of execution.

It has been said often in the golf architectural industry that great holes are a mixture of risk-and-reward. If so, Shinnecock Hills's twelfth hole encapsulates all that is great in a golf hole. I say this both from the playing aspect of the hole, as well as the visual beauty of the surrounds.

The features intrinsic to this hole, and those throughout the entire course for that matter, are outstanding. You won't encounter any 'fancy dan' bunkers on this layout, only large elliptical sand features set into strong, grass faces. These hazards have a certain grandness, one that does not instantly draw the eye to the shape or design. Instead, they fit, as strong features should do, perfectly into the landscape—their scale and style matched to the surrounds into which they are set.

Seemingly, each hole at the Shinnecock Hills is set into its own landscape, prompting the incomparable Ben Hogan to comment: 'Each hole is different and requires a great deal of skill to play properly … all in all I think Shinnecock is one of the finest courses I have played.'

In spite of being British and loving almost all British courses, my views are similar. It has been likened to a British seaside course, although, the careful design of the holes contrasts with the often idiosyncratic challenges that characterise many British seaside courses. However, the twelfth hole at Shinnecock Hills has all the markings of a great hole, namely, strategy, beauty, scale, and challenge.

I recall vividly the first time I played the course one late summer's day. We had finished the round and a mist was beginning to descend upon the course. After a quick drink, we were then ushered gently out of the clubhouse into the crisp evening air. We drove down the driveway and one suddenly had a sense that, while the golfer roamed the course during the day, the original inhabitants—the American Red Indian—returned and reclaimed their mystical and spiritual home at night. Balance restored, I think.

Simon Gidman
International Golf Course Architects
Ascot under Wychwood, Oxford, England

Pebble Beach Golf Links, USA

Seventh hole Cal Olson

As one of the most frequently photographed golf holes in the Pebble Beach area, and the world for that matter, Pebble's par-three, seventh hole offers all the charms of a golf hole that can be both intimidating, yet also highly accommodating. When tackling this iconic hole, half the trick is gaining your composure after being knocked over by the scenery. This is easier said than done! Not infrequently, the tee-shot requires golfers to manufacture a low shot played under the wind to reduce sideways movement of the ball, or, alternatively, a bold, lofted one that hones in on the pin. The weather conditions will surely dictate, and your choice of club may be anything from a driver to a sand-wedge.

Playing on a clear day with a gentle breeze is not the time to become complacent at Pebble Beach. Do so, and the 1919 Neville–Grant layout will bite hard! On the seventh tee, I'm sure many have internalised: 'What's all the fuss about ... I could almost throw my ball under-arm onto the green.' On such a still day, one may be spared the magnificent distraction of the white-capped waves pummelling against the rocks, but there'll be others to contend with.

The green—a small promontory—with glorious Carmel Bay in the background, appears minute, as one plays to a target squeezed in between a grove of trees on the right, and a copse to the left. Much can go wrong: shots that miss the green to the right, or long, will find the ocean or a greenside bunker. Against this backdrop, it's no wonder that many golfers err to the left! But an overcompensation may result in your ball finding the eighth-hole championship tee-box, where you'll face an extremely delicate chip or pitch. If you are fortunate, your 'conservative' tee-shot will catch a greenside bunker. In spite of being so short, the seventh can torture the mind, coming as it does, sandwiched in-between the challenging and difficult sixth hole, and the searching examination of the eighth hole. I find the seventh to be the friendliest of these three great holes.

Maybe so, but it wasn't so friendly during the fourth round of the 1992 US Open. The rain and wind was howling across Pebble and players were living out their worst nightmares. Tom Kite, of course, was carving out one of the most courageous final rounds in memory, standing up to the lashing better than anyone. It is now part of golfing history how, after dragging his punched mid-iron way to the left, Kite chipped in for a birdie two, which must have felt like an eagle, given the number of fours and fives from other contenders. He didn't quite win the event on this hole, but he certainly announced his intentions. In those atrocious conditions, Kite's par round of seventy-two verged on the ridiculous, and one can only imagine the pride that swelled up within Harvey Pennick—his friend, confidant, and lifetime coach.

Selecting a favourite hole is no easy task, especially as there are countless worthy alternatives. Yet, Pebble's seventh hole won out due to its simplicity—seemingly easy, yet difficult. Regardless of the climatic conditions, you must evaluate all the factors, then execute without fear of the consequence. Believe me, that assignment is much easier when sitting at the computer than when out on the course!

The hole requires great imagination; one must 'feel' the shot and proceed to swing naturally. But when you are exhilarated, nervous, and expectant—all at once—who can swing naturally? Golfers are notoriously poor at screening out swing thoughts on the course, such as the latest tip, and for introducing a slight variation to the norm in the promise of a mid-round 'breakthrough.' Such flights of fancy have no place on the seventh hole at Pebble Beach. Go ahead and give it your best shot, and trust the game you brought to the course.

While pinpointing exactly what determines a favourite hole is difficult, I believe that it being a photogenic as well as a challenging hole plays a dual role. Is there a prettier hole in golf than the seventh at Pebble Beach? If so, I'd sure like to visit and play it some time.

Cal Olson Golf Architecture
San Juan Capistrano, California, USA

Par-3
MEN'S: 106 yards
WOMEN'S: 91 yards
DESIGNER: Jack Neville and
Douglas Grant (1918)

The Royal Melbourne Golf Club, Australia

Tenth hole: West Course Michael Clayton

The tenth hole on the famous West Course at Royal Melbourne is a little par-four—just under 280 metres—yet the championship player is confronted from the tee with a multitude of choices of both club selection and line. There is the temptation of a green lying tantalisingly within reach, but players understand that a four is easily attainable by playing two sensible, and largely risk-free, strokes to the undefended parts of the fairway and green. At tournament time, however, rarely will such a defensive strategy leave the player with a short putt for a birdie.

From the tee, the land drops sharply then rises up around a fearsome bunker and turns left toward the small green at the highest point of the hill. Every time one stands on the tee there is much to consider: the season; temperature; how one is playing; the state of the match or the tournament; where the pin is located; and wind direction—all elements conspiring to determine the day's strategy.

Some days the preferred line is directly at the green, but for all but the very longest hitters it is out of reach into the wind, while downwind, it's well nigh impossible to stop the ball on the putting surface. At ordinary courses lacking the severity and sophistication of Royal Melbourne's green complexes, good players care little if they miss a green as there is always a reasonable chance to flip a lofted wedge up close to the flag. Rarely is it that simple at Australia's best course, and it is certainly not the case at the tenth hole.

The bunkers to the right of the green are deep, and the front of the green is protected by a swale that gathers up a pitch coming up even a fraction short of the putting surface. Shots that fly long—both pitches and drives—are severely punished as the shaved bank behind the green is steep in the extreme and it carries the ball more than twenty metres away from the putting surface. During tournaments, of course, the greens at Royal Melbourne are always at their treacherous best and only the finest pitch shots generate enough useful spin to pull the ball up close to the flag.

The most obvious hazard is the huge bunker embedded into the left hillside, which presents a clear choice from the tee for the daring, and there is a daunting area of the sandy ground between the top corner of the bunker and the green. The bold driving option across the bunker and the sandy waste—full of the course's renowned indigenous heath and the marks of those who have gone before—is a shot only for the confident, the desperate, or the foolish.

For players of my generation there was only one possible hero to support and emulate. I first saw the great Spaniard, Severiano Ballesteros, play in the 1978 Australian PGA Championship at Royal Melbourne, a tournament won by the clinical American, Hale Irwin. He took the course apart on the first day and this brilliant round of sixty-four was his most significant of the week. Seve was his antithesis as a player and clinical he was not. He played with a joyous passion and the different approach those two great players bought to the game could not have been better exemplified by another hole in the world.

Irwin and his great friend Graham Marsh played the hole with all their renowned common sense and professionalism. Their long-irons from the tee were hit precisely to the corner of the dogleg, well away from the bunker and they pitched from there. The accurate play of both was legendary and it would have been a surprise had they left themselves with putts longer than four or five paces for their birdies threes. Never was there a risk of either making an annoying and stupid bogey on such a short hole heading into the four-hole stretch of long par-fours—holes at the western end of the Composite Course that are at the heart of its difficulty.

Irwin and Marsh, though, were not the players to attract the big crowds that week. It was the Spaniard who enthralled Melbourne's golfers with his brilliance and flair. Here was a player, barely more than a boy, playing with a carefree abandon proving the ideals of its designer, Alister Mackenzie, were indeed ones to ensure every time we played one of his courses we would fall in love with the game all over again.

Seve arrived at the tenth tee each day and peered with all his charisma at the distant green protected by formidable areas of sand, its shaved banks designed to sweep the ball away, and the front swale. He was born to attempt shots beyond the capabilities of the ordinary professional and one sensed that he understood how disappointed his gallery would have been had he opted for the two-iron, or even a cautious three-wood.

Par-4
MEN'S: 279 Metres
WOMEN'S: 235 Metres
DESIGNER: Alister Mackenzie (1926)

Inevitably, the head-cover came off his biggest club—a beautiful old black Macgregor driver—and he took dead aim at the flag four days straight. Each round he made the most audacious of swings, firing off beautiful and daring shots directly at the green, but it proved beyond the reach of even his best drive. Day after day his ball fell just short of the green into the sandy waste, but that was never a problem for the man with the best short-game any player has ever been blessed with. Like the Pied Piper, the inspired Spaniard led us in our hundreds to the top of the hill to discover what potentially diabolical lie the sand, heath and the footprints had waiting to test his sublime skill. Nothing, though, it seemed, worried Ballesteros. His hands were made for recovery and excitement.

Seve played a succession of brilliant recoveries with his most lofted club, leaving his supporters with memories to last a lifetime. The reward for this boldness, bordering on recklessness, was three birdies and a lone par. While Irwin wrapped up the championship late on the final afternoon, Ballesteros played himself into a respectable third place but he was learning Royal Melbourne and the shots he would need to win there and at Augusta National. Within two years he had won at both 'Cathedrals of Mackenzie', where the reward goes to the golfer exhibiting the greatest touch, nerve, and imagination.

For that short period of time—the end of the seventies to the middle of the eighties—Seve was the master of both Royal Melbourne and Augusta. Alister Mackenzie would have loved it. The Scot had been an admirer of the great Hagen and here, fifty years on, was his reincarnation.

Michael Clayton Golf Design
Melbourne, Victoria, Australia

MICHAEL COCKING 03

ABOVE AND BELOW The Royal Melbourne Golf Club (West):
Third hole, Australia. (Photos by David Scaletti.)

ABOVE Royal Adelaide Golf Club: Third hole, Australia. (Photo by David Scaletti.)
BELOW The Royal Melbourne Golf Club (East): Third hole, Australia. (Photo by David Scaletti.)

ABOVE Victoria Golf Club: Fifteenth hole,
Australia. (Photo by David Scaletti.)

OPPOSITE The Royal Melbourne Golf Club (West):
Tenth hole, Australia. (Photo by David Scaletti.)

Pine Valley Golf Club, USA
First hole Steve Smyers

The designer of Pine Valley, George Crump, was an excellent player in addition to being an extremely creative and intense individual. He held firm opinions on several key aspects of the game: how the game should be played; the rewards a player would receive for a well-thought-out and executed shot; and the penalties they should face following errant play. Most of all, Crump felt that mental labour was as big a part of the game as the physical act of striking of the ball. On every hole at Pine Valley, strategy plus risk-and-reward options operate at a premium, on every shot. Crump not only demanded precise shotmaking on each hole, he required competitors to execute the right shot for the occasion.

To help put all this into context, and maybe catch a glimpse into Crump's mind-set, it is worth remembering that Pine Valley was designed and developed between 1914 and 1918, prior to steel-shafted clubs. One aspect we take for granted today—numbered clubs—had not as yet come into vogue. The fourteen-club limit had not been instituted, and golf balls had very little stability or velocity. All these factors made the game of golf considerably more of a 'ground' game than today, requiring golfers to use their imagination and to trust their natural instincts.

Crump was particularly thoughtful about the first hole, understanding only too well that it may be the nineteenth hole in a play-off. So, he created a great start to one of the world's best golf courses—a great option, risk-and-reward hole. By doing so, he put in train a preview of the decision-making, shotmaking, and strategy, needed to conquer Pine Valley, or at the very least, to be not be too badly battered by it.

The strategy of the par-four, opening hole begins with its green-complex. This large, undulating target is open in the front and can be accessed by a run-up shot. Any shot that finishes to its right, or left, falls away some twenty feet! A miss to either side will surely result in a bogey, or higher.

At first, the tee-shot width appears to be highly forgiving, but as is the case with every tee-shot and approach at Pine Valley, strategy and course management is placed at a premium. Right from the outset, one must make a decision on how to attack this medium-length two-shotter.

The wide, left-to-right, sloping fairway offers several options. One is to take the bold route: challenging the deep, imposing bunker on the inside of the dogleg. From here, a short-iron from the preferred lie, and angle, can be played. The safe play from the tee is to the left—the safest side of the fairway—leaving a mid- to long-iron second, from a downhill lie. And then, golfers have an important decision to make. Depending on the direction of the wind, firmness of the ground, lie of the ball, and hole location, golfers can either place their faith in the aerial route to the green, or play the ball short and rely upon a good bounce forward. For many golfers, the safest play would be to lay-up, taking all the trouble out of the equation, and then positioning oneself for a crafty 'up-and-down' par.

In the many competitive rounds I have played at this remarkable course, I've witnessed some of the most accomplished amateur golfers in America post scores from three to nine, in almost every event. One comes to expect a range of scores—poles apart—no doubt, uncontrollable nerves play their part. Perhaps some golfers have read too much into the legendary Pine Valley 'needle.'

I have always been enamoured with the beauty, design, and playability of this hole. If you will be lenient and allow a brief personal digression, the hole will always remain at the forefront of my mind for being the hole where my longest-running, and best golfing accomplishment took place. During a better-ball event, I somehow managed to birdie this hole on five consecutive occasions: twice in the Medal-play portion of the event, and three times in the Match-play section. A personal best!

Though Crump is credited with Pine Valley's design, much credit should also be accorded to Harry S. Colt, the outstanding British architect who designed many well-known courses in the British Isles.

Colt led Crump in the routing and overall planning of the course. Such was the magnetic appeal of Crump, Pine Valley, and potential of its fabulous golfing terrain, that several other designers dropped by to share their ideas on design. Showcasing a veritable who's who of golf course design, those to put forth opinions included Walter Travis, who designed Garden City Men's Club, Henry C. Fownes who created Oakmont, and A. W. Tillinghast of Winged Foot and San Francisco Golf Club fame. Indeed, it was Tillinghast's risk-and-reward

design philosophy that helped influence the building of Pine Valley's thirteenth hole. Englishman, Charles H. Alison, who was Colt's partner, also had input. George Crump enlisted the opinions of these brilliant men, but in the final analysis, it was his own imagination and genius that created one of golf's masterpieces.

Steve Smyers Golf Course Architects
Lakeland, Florida, USA

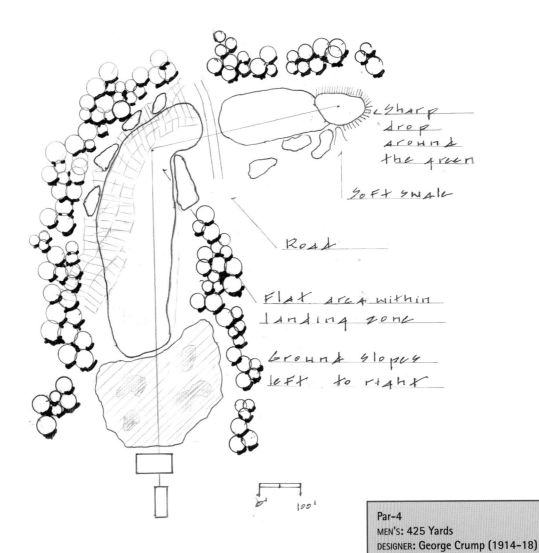

Sharp drop around the green

90 Ft swale

Road

Flat area within landing zone

Ground slopes left to right

100'

Par-4
MEN'S: 425 Yards
DESIGNER: George Crump (1914–18)

Leven Links, Scotland
Eighteenth hole Dr Martin Hawtree

Leven Links lies on the celebrated Fife Coast, overlooking Largo Bay on the Firth of Fourth, as one of a string of fine Scottish courses that ring Fife from St. Andrews on the east, round past Crail and Elie, to Lundin and Leven in the south. Lundin and Leven once shared nine holes of each of their present courses, as the single original golf course stretching the two miles between the respective clubhouses. That was in 1868. The links in its present form dates from 1909.

The final holes at Leven present a superlative run of golf, although, they were once a good deal more testing than now, when the railway line ran eerily within a few yards of the thirteenth, fourteenth, and fifteenth holes. Generally played into the prevailing wind, this stretch was a heroic trio of a par-five, a -four, and a -three. The sixteenth hole continues the run into the wind, but is less burdensome being a shorter par-four. After departing the sixteenth green there is another turn, and players welcome the respite of the medium-length, down-wind seventeenth hole. And not before time! There is time to gather one's composure, and gather it one must. For the final hole at Leven Links is back into the prevailing wind, and it's as fine an eighteenth hole as you likely to come across: a 457-yard par-four over rolling fairway that is shared with the first hole. One must give a wide berth to the concealed, steep clefts on the left-hand side that easily gathers up the drives turning excessively to the left. Troublesome rough awaits a wayward drive to the right, and, ahead, one notices a veritable mirage of wood and grass on the horizon. Clearly, this hole is not for the lily-livered. But the player does know what is in store, having stood on the first tee—only a few hours before—just feet away from what appears the most treacherous green imaginable.

Mercifully, the green is generous in size: much more so than the original small square green. Announcing itself like two end-to-end cricket pitches, it is forty yards in length and thirty yards wide, situated on what your brain tells your eyes is an impossible slope: falling through a full metre in height, from back-left, to front-right. The slope is fierce at the back: 1:24 across the back-left quadrant; 1:12 along the left side; easing to 1:40 on the front, right-hand side. Visually, the green seems to slide naturally up to the front of the clubhouse, echoing the strong vertical element of the building. It is a green that Alister Mackenzie must surely have been conscious of in some of his Australian work, with the size, slope, and feature, pushed right to the limit.

The slope is indeed fundamental to the hole working at all. A few feet from the front edge of the green, and working its way around the right-hand side, there is a sudden drop to an imposing wooden retaining wall. Golfers: meet Scoonie Burn—one of the most notorious burns in Links golf. From around this green, one cannot entertain thoughts of playing a grandstand traditional links bump-and-run: it is all, or nothing. Thank heavens for the slope.

The burn is the crux of the hole. The scattering of bunkers along the fairway, and the deep clefts over on the left do not really prey on the mind of the player on the tee. The focus is in getting a long drive away—as close to the distant burn as possible—to enable a second shot to the green without complete deflation of spirit. That element of pressure and challenge should affect all players, which is one legitimate reason why the hole should not be lengthened. Take the burn out of sensible reach and challenge for the average golfer, and there is no challenge at all.

With the eighteenth green bordering on the limits of acceptable slope, protected by the most absolute of watery defences around more than a third of the green's perimeter, and being a long hole played into the teeth of the prevailing wind—as well as a winter setting sun—sees the eighteenth hole as an implausible challenge. If you need anything else to ratchet up the difficulty stakes another notch, Out of bounds, in the form of a bowling green lurks not that many yards to the right of the eighteenth green. All around there is potential for disaster, but it is somehow miraculously transformed into a truly satisfying finishing hole, elevating the spirits rather than casting them down. And spirits should be high, playing homeward toward the craggy outline of the town of Leven, and the two, fine, welcoming clubhouses of the Leven Golfing Society and the Leven Thistle Golf Club.

Hawtree Limited
Woodstock, Oxford, England

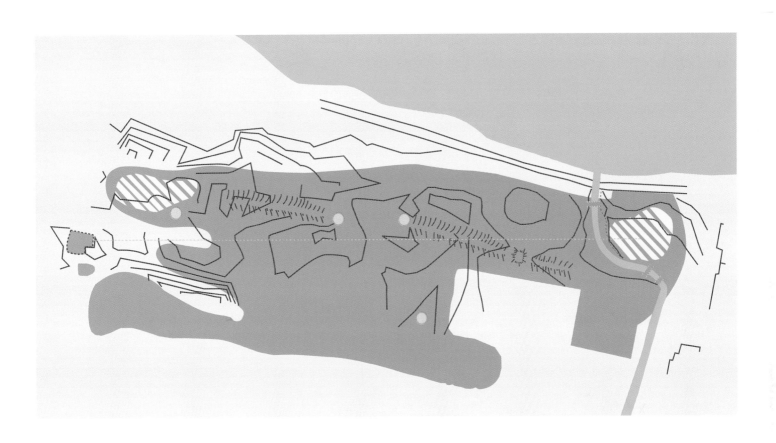

Par-4
MEN'S: 457 Yards
WOMEN'S: 445 Yards (Par 5)
DESIGNER: A. Patrick (1909)

The Australian Golf Club, Australia

Eighteenth hole Bob Shearer

Designed by Hutchinson, Martin, and Clark, The Australian Golf Club opened in 1905. Alister Mackenzie was in Australia to design Royal Melbourne in 1926, providing The Australian with an opportunity of securing his services for advice. Indeed, the Sydney-based club was one of the nineteen, or so, Antipodean clubs to avail itself of his services. Mackenzie-inspired changes naturally took place. In 1977, a further upgrade was undertaken at The Australian, when the 'inner' course disappeared as part of Jack Nicklaus's redesign.

Nicklaus dramatically changed this famous course. New holes were constructed, lakes were added, hybrid Bermuda fairways replaced the Kikuyu, and the nines were reversed, offering a panoramic view of the eighteenth hole with its natural amphitheatre from the clubhouse.

The par-five, eighteenth hole is one of the most intriguing, finishing holes in Australian golf, and in spite of its moderate length—only 475 metres—it creates a variety of challenges for all golfers.

Hitting a straight tee-shot is of maximum importance, due to the presence of a large, deep bunker situated on the right-hand side of the fairway at 233 metres from the tee. It guards the undulating and narrow fairway, and for any golfer whose drive strays into this hazard, a defensive lay-up is their only option.

If the drive has been struck straight and true, the longer hitter must make a calculated decision on whether to attempt the long carry to the narrow, three-tiered green. Water lies in the front and right of the green, and there is a deep bunker to its left. There are troublesome hazards all around, leaving the golfer with an inspiring second shot with a long-iron, or fairway metal—a genuine test of skill and nerve. To miss the green to the right will signal a watery grave; to be conservative and miss to the left means the golfer will face a difficult bunker shot, or a treacherous chip-shot, to a firm and fast green with the water tantalisingly in view.

If circumstances dictate that a lay-up after the drive is prudent, such a shot must be played with careful calculation. Water on the right stretches back ninety metres short of the green, while cleverly placed fairway bunkers on the left, alerts the player to the need of being precise. Above all, one must play with conviction if hoping to avoid these hazards. Successful negotiation of the lay-up should benefit the golfer with a good third-shot line and length: important considerations in order to play an attacking, firm pitch to the flagstick.

There are no hidden obstacles on this fine, finishing hole: golfers can easily view what is in front of them. But will their nerve, temperament, and skill, hold up with the decision they make?

During the twentieth century, the club played host to many Australian Opens, plus countless Australian professional and amateur tournaments. Over the years, there have been many memorable finishes played out here, and one that comes to mind is the 1982 Australian Open: I only wish I still had the same nerve now!

But, I am sure there will be more dramatic and exciting finishes on this challenging, closing hole in years to come.

Shearer Golf Design
Melbourne, Victoria, Australia

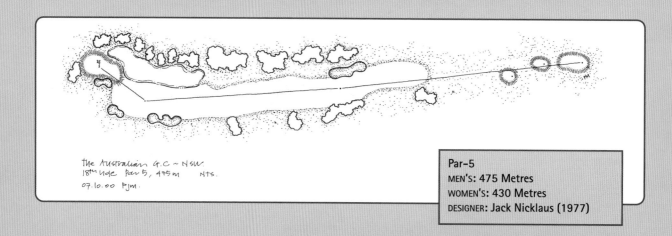

the Australian G.C ~ NSW.
18th hole Par 5, 475m   Nts.
07.10.00 PJM.

Par-5
MEN'S: 475 Metres
WOMEN'S: 430 Metres
DESIGNER: Jack Nicklaus (1977)

Banff Springs Golf Club, Canada

Fourth hole Jeff Howes

My favourite golf hole is the 192-yard par-three, fourth hole at Banff Springs, Canada. It goes by the name of 'Devil's Cauldron.' Located in Banff, Alberta, the course opened for play in 1927, and must surely be the envy of nearly all others, being laid out in one of the most geographically stupendous settings in the world.

The hole was designed by the famous Canadian golf-course architect Stanley Thompson. It has been said that he was a genius at designing par-threes, and one wonders what masterful designs the golf world was deprived of following his premature passing in 1952 at the age of fifty-eight. In this beautiful but harsh environment construction is dear. Indeed, Thompson's course holds the unusual distinction of being the first in the world to cost more than one million dollars to build.

Banff's fourth hole has everything, and is golf on a grand scale. The tee-shot is downhill, to a green perched on a shelf on the opposite side of a glacial lake. Somewhat eerily, the water in the lake is so crystal clear that golf balls lying on the bottom of the lake remain visible. Playing the fourth, you almost hope that no one is present: to hit just one solitary ball from this lofty peak is the equivalent of golfing cruelty. You'd much prefer to relieve your bag of its balls, and just unload. It's nice to dream. Back to golf: Mt. Rundle makes an awe-inspiring backdrop. The green slopes from back-to-front, and is surrounded by bunkers. Not only do the elevated tees make club-selection difficult, the swirling wind makes the playing challenge reminiscent of the twelfth hole at Augusta National—in its ability to confuse golfers and impact upon club selection, not in looks.

The sheer beauty of the location is enhanced by Thompson's clever manipulation, through his design, of the player's mind. Ever so thoughtfully, the bunkers surrounding the green are shaped to mimic the natural, ragged-edged, snowy slopes of Mt. Rundle.

J. Howes

When playing the fourth hole at Banff Springs, the magnitude of the mountains, the view of the crystal clear water below, and the total feeling of isolation combine beautifully to present the total golf experience. Come and play Banff Springs and join the chorus: this is golf and nature at its best.

Jeff Howes Golf Design Ltd
Kilkenny, Ireland

Par–3
MEN'S: 192 Yards
WOMEN'S: 79 Yards
DESIGNER: Stanley Thompson (1927)

Oakmont Country Club, USA

Fourth hole Jeffrey D. Brauer

I especially like holes where the features are memorable and colourfully ascribed. The heart stirs when one hears names synonymous with great golf happenings of the past. Names such as: 'Road,' 'Punchbowl,' 'Bottleneck,' 'Dell,' 'Island,' or even, 'Maxwell's Rolls.' But not all happenings are great: these names are highly indicative of the history of titanic struggles between golfers and golf course.

At Oakmont Country Club, no feature is more memorable than the famous 'Church Pews'—a large fairway bunker that separates the third and fourth fairways. The bunker contains several rows of grassy hummocks, and is every bit as fearsome as its reputation.

While the third hole attracts the most publicity, I far prefer the fourth. Players like holes for many reasons. Better players like holes that require the shots to be easily envisioned; average 'weekend' players love famous holes at exclusive clubs; golf-course architects like unique features; while golf historians are known to swoon over the less-heralded gems, which may display design themes of the past. To underscore the brilliance of Oakmont's fourth hole, it displays elements that appeal to each of the above.

When standing upon the fourth tee, the task at hand requires little guesswork. The tee-shot is well defined, as safe negotiation of the Church Pews, in combination with stacked bunkers on the right-hand side, clearly calls for a controlled shot that drifts gently from left to right.

The second shot also requires the same shaping, and allows players to determine their own strategy, rather than the usual par-five pre-requisite of merely advancing the ball as far as possible! One does, however, have to be mindful of two clusters of fairway bunkers on the right of the second landing area. The second-shot dilemma is how to get as near to these bunkers as possible without actually visiting them; the green is very narrow, and angled from that direction, making it much more receptive to shots from that region. The green narrows toward the back, making the decision on your second shot very tricky when the pin is located at the rear of the green.

While playing Oakmont's fourth hole, you cannot help being aware of its unique place in US golf-course design, and what a profound influence it has exerted during tournaments, most famously, US Opens. It is hardly a stretch to say: a course like this—designed by Henry C. Fownes in 1904—will never be built again.

Perhaps one reason for this assertion is that the course is shamelessly penal. Historians and students of golf-course architecture are quick to outline how 'Golden-Age' design theories of angles of play were inspired in response to Oakmont's difficulty. There may be an element of truth in this, but the hole also demonstrates that it is a shining example of two schools of thought.

Coincidently, while the hole appears timeless, and unchanged, it has in fact endured its fair share of modification over the years, namely: a rebuilt green; some bunkers rebuilt; and extended tees, to keep its notorious Church Pew 'in play' for modern golf professionals. The first-hand evidence shows that everything has blended in astonishingly well.

Like most average golfers, I found that playing Oakmont was a rare and wonderful treat. Indeed, I did find myself 'up close and personal' with the famous Church Pews following my tee-shot, which went left as if drawn by a magnet. It was among its clutches that I found myself replicating the famous picture of Arnold Palmer trying to recover on the third hole. I had my struggles, but the experience did furnish me with a golfing story to tell. My plight naturally gave rise to some good-natured bantering from my grinning opponent, and my caddie, along the lines of: 'Should have spent more time in Church last week, Jeff—closest you'll ever get to playing like Palmer—I'm praying for you—You'll do some penance now!' And on they went, at my expense.

But having lived to tell the tale, my story brings out the empathetic streak inherent in golfers—'knowing nods'—having themselves battled an instantly recognised and famous adversary called the Church Pews. And memories such as those are what really creates favourite holes.

Jeffrey D. Brauer/GolfScapes, Inc
Arlington, Texas, USA

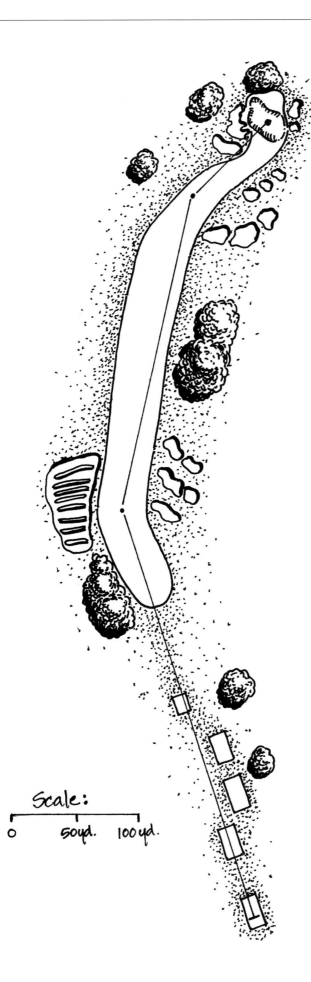

'Church Pews'
Par-5
MEN'S: 621 Yards
WOMEN'S: 467 Yards
DESIGNER: Henry C. Fownes (1903)

Scale:

0   50yd.   100yd.

Royal Montreal Golf Club, Canada

Sixteenth hole: Blue Course Jeremy Glenn

Royal Montreal—North America's oldest golf club, founded in 1873—is where one of golf's most notorious battlegrounds resides: a Cape-style, 433-yard beast lurking near the end of the round with an approach shot you worry about on the first tee, and a driving challenge that kept you awake the night before.

As with the first volley of any duel, in this case the sixteenth hole's tee-shot, you simply hope to keep your ball on the short grass, as anything to the left of the fairway is a dark sea of shattered dreams. But disaster's proximity to greatness is rarely this sharply defined: a shoreline so frightening yet so tempting to dare. From the tee, golfers will struggle with the inner battle of courage and fear. The meek will see their ball sweeping away in a grandiose yet cowardly arc toward the right, away from the water. From the right of the fairway you are at the mercy of the rough and sentinel trees, with the green beckoning from atop a distant hill, so inviting yet beyond reach of all but the mightiest blow. The smartest play is therefore to hit a short-iron down the fairway, short of the water, followed by another short-iron to the green. With consistent if unspectacular play, one could make a five on this hole even under the most demanding pressure. But it is so difficult to resist such a tempting reward, to bite off a little more, to hit the ball just that little bit further. Thus, golfers either by greed or false bravery, will reach to the top of their bag and aim for the distant shore, vying to leave themselves a short pitch or chip and a crack at a patchy, but legitimate, par. Yet, in so doing, they bring the water into play on the second shot, as it lurks thirty yards short of the green and to the right of it. 'If I must fail,' they seem to admit, 'let it be in a grandiose way.'

On the other hand, whether courageous or foolish, a powerful tee-shot down the fairway's left-hand side taunts the hazard while safely bounding alongside of it, like a Machiavellian child in front of the lion's cage. But such a courageous line must be struck with authority as well as accuracy, as the carry to the fairway lengthens for the bold, and encroaching trees to the right will ensnare the long-hitter who doubts their convictions. But success reaps its just reward: a great drive leaves a simple mid-iron or even less, into the large green, from where a solid approach can see the golfer gain one, if not two, strokes on the field.

That's not to say the sixteenth hole is perfect. The bunker short-left of the green adds little to the hole. Its location is arbitrary, without relation to the land or the shots at hand, while its physical appearance is far from memorable. Yet such a petty criticism cannot take away from the intimidating merit of this golf hole. Its features and their relation to one another, put in place both by nature and by design, provide the stage for one of the greatest golf holes in the country. It allows reprieve for those who decline the challenge, at the cost of a stroke. Yet it entices so mischievously those who wish to save that stroke, and punishes ruthlessly should they unsuccessfully succumb to that temptation.

Graham Cooke & Associates Inc.
Beaconsfield, Quebec, Canada

Par-4
MEN'S: 433 Yards
WOMEN'S: 317 Yards
DESIGNER: Dick Wilson (1957)

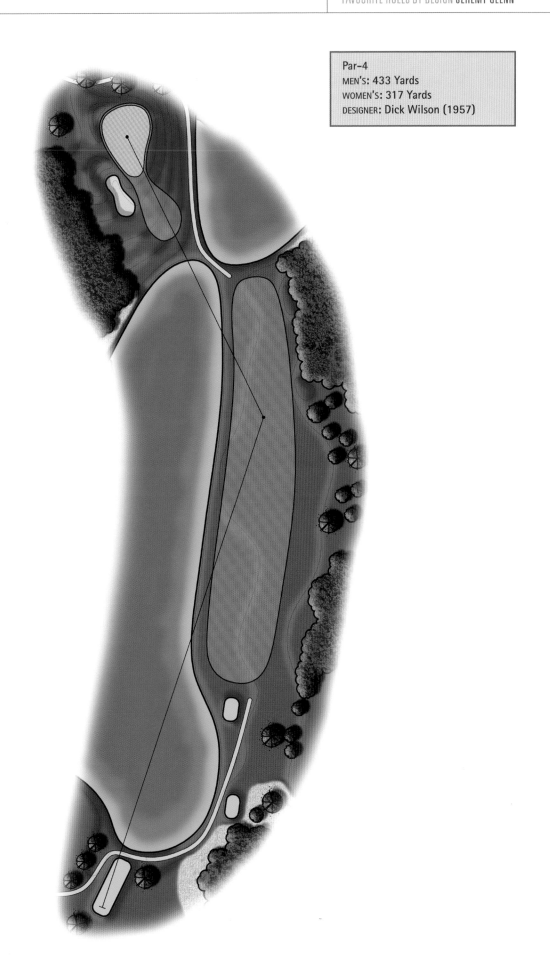

Holyhead Golf Club, North Wales
First hole Ian Scott-Taylor

Holyhead in North Wales lies on the west tip of Anglesey, and is commonly referred to as: 'The gateway to Ireland.' Courtesy of the railway companies of the era, golf was spreading across the country in the early part of the twentieth century. Holyhead was the main steam packet and Royal Mail port for Ireland, and it figured highly in Britain's infrastructure and economy of the day. Upon completion of the new railway station and hotel, James Braid—five-times Open Champion—was commissioned to craft a links for the railway company on land that boarded the coastline on the west of Holy Island.

Not only could he play, Braid was some designer, and his Holyhead layout is a classic. He saw to it that there was an abundance of holes with wonderful shotmaking opportunities, and holes that utilised the natural terrain and elements to create a walker's dream on the sea. Although short at only 6,000 yards, when the gales of the Irish Sea blow, they turn this links into a championship examination for any professional tour player: even Tiger Woods.

Granted, it is acknowledged as a shotmaker's delight, but it's also the ideal place to learn how to play and cope with the wind. During any such apprenticeship, one does learn how to manage the course. As for the wind, there is no respite: it blows every day. A wrong choice of club, or strategy, and the golfing gods wreak their wrath and show no mercy.

At only 277 yards from the 'tips', the first is an unusually short opener, with nary a bunker in sight. As you stand on the tee, the eighth green is stationed nearby to your right, as the eighth hole runs parallel to the first in the opposite direction. And not far behind the first tee is where the eighteenth green lies. You'd be within your rights to be feeling slightly claustrophobic by now. Perhaps adding to any feeling of being hemmed-in is the knowledge that the clubhouse is just to the left of the first tee, and above you. For a Wednesday Alliance Tournament, or in the Saturday Medal, the fence is lined with golfing spectators watching your first drive to the fairway, or your bold attempt to drive the green, should you possess the nerve. There is nowhere to hide. By comparison, the nerve-wracking drive off Merion's first tee is a doddle.

Other than being scared out of your wits, the first thing that draws your attention is the view; the green is 'blind' and hidden behind a large mound that masks the target. The only indication of the green's general vicinity is the seven-foot flag that marks the prize that awaits all.

For mere mortals, the hole plays as a short, par-four. For the accomplished golfer, though, it really does beckon a birdie start. However, if the drive is faulty in any manner, the bogey side of golf opens up surprisingly easily. The placement of one's tee-shot is always the key to scoring. Right off the bat at Holyhead, this aspect demands attention, especially with an Out of bounds stonewall to the left. This is not the time and place to suddenly slip in a snap-hook. But golfers are more likely to carve one away, and take up residence on the adjoining eighth fairway. In spite of its short length, second shots demand 'local' knowledge, skill, and a fearless heart. Visitors may be blissfully ignorant, but members know one fact only too well: the green, which falls away from the incoming shot, increases the difficulty of approaching.

Most players drive to the top of the hill, which is a small plateau. At this point, you can almost feel players' nerves starting to jangle upon finding out that greenkeeper, Gwilym Roberts, has placed the flag in the front portion of the green: a most awkward location. While the drive is one that can wipe the smile off your face, it's the second to the green that determines whether it's to be an easy par, or impressive birdie. Accuracy and judgment is at a premium here: a misjudged or mistimed approach short of the green, or a push, will see the ball catch the bank in front of the green. Even from such close range, golfers will be faced with a most difficult recovery for par.

The green is small—only 4,500 square feet—and typical of Braid. It is laden with more subtle breaks than I care to mention, with some flat areas of a mere one per cent in certain places. Old James inserted one other fiendish item: a ridge that runs from left to right diagonally across the green. With such a prominent feature, any first putt not struck with authority, ends up in three-putt territory: a not uncommon scenario for me.

To further complicate matters, the green is set in a dell with gorse to its left, and topography that seems to funnel and magnify the wind.

In spite of its modest length, the first at Holyhead is a hole of many stories. I'd be delighted to hear on the 'grapevine' some day, that perhaps as a result of this essay, you made a visit to the course as part of your journey through to Ireland. It won't disappoint, I can promise you that.

Ian Scott-Taylor
Golf Course Architect
Easton, Maryland, USA

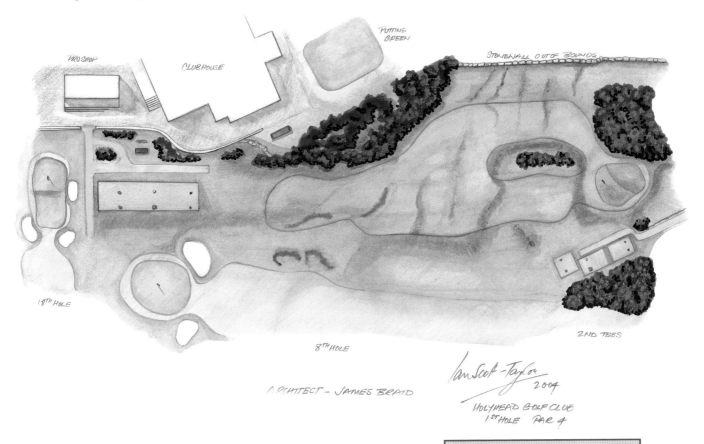

Par-4
MEN'S: 277 Yards
WOMEN'S: 255 Yards
DESIGNER: James Braid (1911)

ABOVE Durban Country Club: Second hole, South Africa.
by Larry Lambrecht, LC Lambrecht Photography.)

OPPOSITE ABOVE National Golf Links of America: Third hole, USA.
(Photo by Larry Lambrecht, LC Lambrecht Photography.)

OPPOSITE BELOW National Golf Links of America: Seventeenth hole, USA.
(Photo by Larry Lambrecht, LC Lambrecht Photography.)

Royal Worlington and Newmarket Golf Club, England

Fifth hole Martin Ebert

Many of the world's most acclaimed golf holes wring out a similar human response: while standing on the tee, the air of nervous anticipation is all around. That is most definitely the case on the par-three, fifth hole at Royal Worlington and Newmarket Golf Club. Although no more than 155 yards distant, the thin sliver of green appears to be an almost impossible haven to hit; holding your ball on its surface is another matter entirely.

Royal Worlington is remarkable for several aspects: not the least for being a thought-provoking and excellent nine-hole layout. A striking aspect is that the course is situated on a parcel of land no more than about forty acres: one that is brimming with quality golf of the traditional kind. To explain how the course fits within such tight confines is easy: some holes cross each other. The tee-shot on the third hole is played over the second green, the eighth hole drive skirts the seventh green, the ninth hole plays over a public road, while the fifth hole actually crosses over the fourth green and the line of the sixth hole tee-shot! Yet another factor that compounds the difficulty of the fifth hole tee-shot: there always seems to be a gathering of golfers keen to see how you fair.

Regarding the internal course features, you would be hard pressed to determine what is natural and what is not—a goal that all golf-course architects should aspire to. There is always a need to carry out some reshaping, of course, but the master designer and construction crew work toward making any sign of reshaping difficult to detect. 'Worlie' is a real masterpiece in this respect.

Being home to the Cambridge University Golf Club, I first discovered the course when selected for a team trial match, and we headed off one very foggy morning. Fortuitously, I was paired with someone who knew the course reasonably well. He pointed me in the right direction on the outward nine, and I was pleasantly surprised when I reached the turn at a respectable one or two over par. However, the fog lifted, and so did my score for the inward nine. That may have been a result of being able to see the hazards that the course possessed. On reflection, the fifth hole was a much easier prospect on that first meeting; being obscured from any sight of the green, I simply could not see the horrors awaiting anything but the finest of blows.

Now to describe those horrors: the first thing to convey is that it is a hole without a single bunker in play. The contours of the terrain from tee to green, plus the shape of the green and its contours, provide more than enough protection. As I have alluded to previously, the green is extremely narrow. It is maybe no more than six or seven paces wide, and on both sides the land falls away severely—down to Mug's Hollow on the left, named after all of the mugs who have fallen foul of it—and away to a stream, which is really too far away to be a hazard, on the right.

Those who have played the hole a number of times will have invariably experienced the humbling act of playing from one side of the green, to the other. One famous story tells of a renowned foursomes pair finding the target in one shot, putting off with their second, and remaining off the green after nine more! Yet recoveries can be played by striking chip-and-run shots aggressively into the green's tightly cut bank, thereby, allowing the ball clamber up and over the edge of the green. You are not forced to 'lob' the ball all the way onto the surface—a rather tiresome characteristic of many modern courses—although I doff my hat to anyone who has the nerve and skill to attempt such an approach. Finding the green with a recovery shot from either side of the green, feels almost as satisfying as finding the putting surface with your tee-shot!

Some time ago, Donald Steel offered an appropriate assessment of the green's surface. He likened it to a 'vaulting horse.' The green rises for some thirty-five yards through a series of steep slopes, which define a number of small shelves—some flatter than others. Legitimate flagstick positions are limited on this green, but that does not adversely impact upon the quality of the putting surface. Like all of the greens at

Par-3
MEN'S: **155 Yards**
WOMEN'S: **140 Yards**
DESIGNER: **Tom Dunn (1893)**

Worlington—renowned as some of Britain's finest in wintertime—the fifth green remains dry and firm throughout the year.

The fifth hole at Royal Worlington and Newmarket Golf Club takes us back to a bygone era, and everyone who has tackled its many nuances develops a soft spot for its 'old-world' charms. The extremity of some of its features would be difficult to justify in today's golfing environment, but there are lessons to be learnt and applied. What makes it so much fun is the prospect of one pure stroke from the tee, seeing your ball come to rest nearby the flag. And being a nine-hole course, there are two tantalising opportunities per round to sample its delights!

Donald Steel & Company Ltd
International Golf Course Architects
Chichester, West Sussex, England

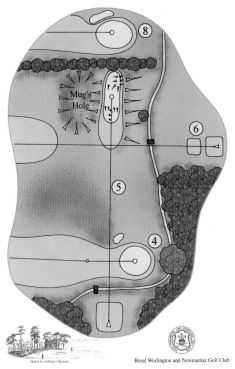

Royal Worlington and Newmarket Golf Club

Victoria Golf Club, Australia
Fifteenth hole Michael Cocking

Melbourne's sandbelt region is famed for its courses, and, in part, the number of world-class, short par-fours. One only has to play holes such as Royal Melbourne's tenth hole (West), Kingston Heath's third, Woodlands' intriguing third and fourth holes, Long Island's eighth, and the new thirteenth hole at Peninsula North, to appreciate what heights golf-course architecture can reach. Through inspired green design and bunkering, these holes are challenging, yet, remain eminently playable for all ages and skill levels.

My favourite short four, however, is the 296-metre fifteenth hole at Victoria Golf Club. Scarcely can I think of another hole where a player's game is so heavily scrutinised on the tee, or a hole that presents as many options.

Situated atop a long, skinny ridge, much of the playing difficulty lies in negotiating a series of bunkers carved out along the left side of the fairway. Visually confronting, they tease and taunt golfers of varying abilities; for if the ball can be hit directly over, or manoeuvred from right to left, the reward may be the rare opportunity of an eagle putt. This daring tee-shot, however, easily carries the most risk, with the fairway at its widest before the start of the bunkers, and narrowing the closer one gets to the green.

Some golfers will instinctively 'chance their arm' by reaching for the driver, but conventional wisdom usually dictates that a long-iron be played into position. Remarkably, though, anything from a six-iron to a driver, can be played from the tee legitimately, depending upon pin position, wind direction, the state of your game, and how much risk you are willing to take.

By Melbourne standards, the green is small. It slopes from front to back and is angled to favour play from the left, although a pin placed just over the front-left greenside bunker will reverse the tee-shot strategy, instead favouring the player who hugs the fairway's right-hand side. In typical sandbelt style, the greenside bunkers 'pinch' the putting surface, thereby, creating a number of exciting approach shots that reward short-iron confidence, and the ability to hit precise distances.

In the worst-case scenario—your tee shot finding trouble—the odds of scrounging a par is definitely reduced, but by no means over. Unlike a water-hazard, which Bobby Jones likened to a plane crash (where the result is final), the occasion of your ball in these bunkers could be likened to a car accident, where there is a chance of recovery. While infinitely more difficult than playing from the fairway, imaginative sand play, combined with a touch of skill (or luck) can sometimes salvage a par—perhaps even a birdie if the long bunker shot can be perfectly executed.

The origins of this gem remain largely unknown. While it is commonly acknowledged the course was routed by club secretary Bill Meader and Oscar Damon during the early part of the 1920s, a recently uncovered article suggests the club made significant alterations to the course not long after Dr Alister Mackenzie visited to consult on design and bunker positioning during his whirlwind tour of 1926—when Royal Melbourne enticed him to sail to Australia and design its course. Unfortunately, no documentation exists today to clarify whether Mackenzie made any recommendations to this hole, or, if he did, to what extent these were implemented. Conjecture aside, as an exponent and admirer of strategic holes and golf course design, and one who encouraged bold and imaginative play, it is safe to say that were he not responsible for the design of Victoria's fifteenth hole, he would have surely approved.

Michael Clayton Golf Design
Melbourne, Victoria, Australia

Par-4
MEN'S: 296 Metres
WOMEN'S: 271 Metres
DESIGNERS: Oscar Damman and Bill Meader (1923)

Crystal Downs Country Club, USA
Sixth hole Mike DeVries

The sixth at Crystal Downs is my favourite hole for a variety of reasons: it has the best fairway bunker complex in the world; the best green in the world; and the contour of the land combined with varying winds make its play interesting every day.

Being a short par-four, sandwiched between two other great short fours, it makes for a run of holes that appear to be quite score-enhancing, yet you rarely go through them with three straight pars, or in par, or better. The variety in the three holes provides an endless amount of interest; in fact, you could play the three in continuous succession without ever tiring of the plays.

From its original tee at 351 yards, the regular player is asked to carry a deep valley that cuts across the fifth through eighth holes. The crest of the opposing hill requires a 180-yard drive to safely stay up top, otherwise your ball will roll back down into the valley, leaving an approach of 190–230 yards from a very awkward, uneven stance. Two large oaks border the left side, while a big maple on the right plays havoc with a pushed shot, or drive, that tries to 'cut the corner' too much. The sight line to the green is directly over the 'Scabs' bunker complex, tiered into the hillside just to the right of the maple. The Scabs are narrow, sloping benches in the hillside with rugged grass surrounding them and a large birch and small apple tree on the right of them. When caught within the Scabs' clutches, most players are not lucky enough, or sufficiently skilled, to advance their ball into a decent position to make a play at the hole. The Scabs extract a full stroke penalty—a real hazard in an age when golfers expect to be able to reach the green from any predicament.

From the back tee, better players will have to strike a good drive to safely reach the top of the hill and to be in a position to attack the flagstick. The wind at Crystal Downs is everpresent and blows hard either behind or against you. Driving with the wind would seem to be the easier task, but the added knowledge that you don't have to press to reach the top of the hill sometimes lulls the golfer into a false sense of security and their drive leaves them with a very demanding second shot. When approaching, the golfer can be greeted with a stance from any angle and from any type of grass, as there is fairway, rough, and long, native rough all in play from the tee. A good drive can leave as little as a wedge to the green, but a misplayed drive may leave a long-iron, or fairway metal, from an abrupt lie.

This is a hole where big-hitters have a distinct advantage: they can carry the hill, but beyond the crest is undulating ground that can yield good lies, or awkward stances. From the left-hand side—about sixty yards from the green—is a large ridge that can block the player's view of the target from the valley. Also, a patch of long rough just past the Scabs snares its share of the big-hitters' wayward drives, and frequently those are greeted by a questionable lie. All together, these elements provide numerous playing challenges, and diversity, even in today's technologically advanced game.

The green is the largest on the course and positioned a considerable distance from the two approach bunkers and rear bunker, giving ample room for difficult approaches, and the short game. The contouring of the green is dominated by a large, central bump that will affect all approach shots and seemingly every putt. The back of the green is severely pitched to the middle. The left-hand portion has a narrow shelf

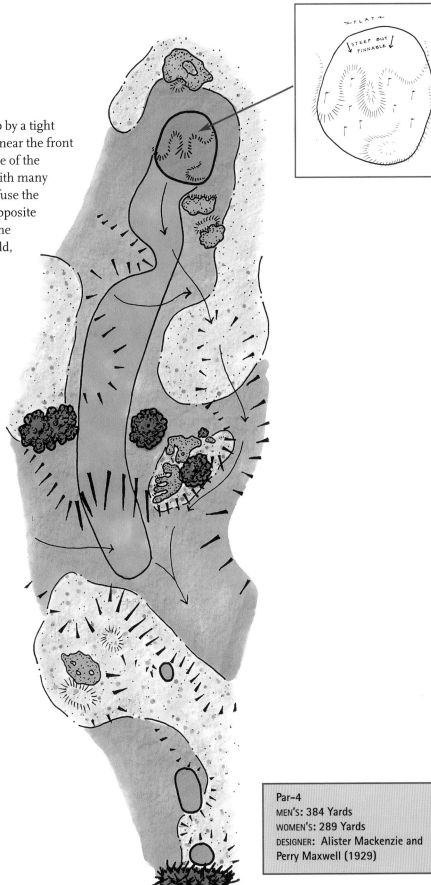

that is separated from the bump by a tight valley that fans out and flattens near the front of the green. The right-hand side of the green features a large plateau with many fine undulations that often confuse the golfer and turn the ball in the opposite direction. It is certainly one of the finest green surfaces in the world, and one that offers an endless variety of pin positions.

The final reason the sixth is my favourite hole is purely personal: as a twelve-year-old I had my first birdie on the Downs at the sixth, playing with my grandmother from the forward tee. As if only yesterday, I recall hitting my drive to the top of the hill and then striking a six-iron approach to six feet below the hole. The memory of draining a smooth putt into the heart of the cup remains vivid. And so does my grandmother's interesting response: 'Well, that's pretty good, why don't we call it a day?' And so we did! Sentimentally, the sixth at Crystal Downs will always be my favourite hole.

DeVries Designs, Inc.
Traverse City, Michigan, USA

Par-4
MEN'S: 384 Yards
WOMEN'S: 289 Yards
DESIGNER: Alister Mackenzie and Perry Maxwell (1929)

Royal Aberdeen Golf Club, Scotland
Ninth hole Niall Glen

Situated on the North East coast of Scotland by the City of Aberdeen, lies the Royal Aberdeen Golf Club. It is only the discerning golf visitor, who, after thoroughly researching Scotland's many and varied links, is likely to stumble upon this gem. The rest, no doubt, will have already rushed north to the overcrowded courses at Cruden Bay and Dornoch, and on their return trip south, bypass the Aberdeen links to make their tee time at Carnoustie.

The famous saying: 'A club's greatest asset is its course,' is something that the members' at Royal Aberdeen take to heart. Traditionally, they have not been too heavily involved in the promotion and marketing of their course, instead preferring to let the course talk for itself. Indeed, you won't find any road signs directing you to the course—a cunning ploy by the members to ensure that this course remains as it was intended to be: a members' course. Yet, this is no stuffy club: any visitor that does arrive here will receive a warm and friendly welcome, and they'll pit their skills with a noble links guaranteed to test every department of their game and temperament.

At Royal Aberdeen, attention is inevitably focused on the outward nine, and it is generally accepted that this half is more spectacular than the inward nine. Each of the first eight holes weaves a meandering trail through the high sand dunes until you reach the ninth hole or, as it is known, 'End.' What awaits you is, in my opinion, something quite special.

To finish the outward half, players encounter a brutal 465-yard par-four. Usually, though, the prevailing wind is assisting the player. From any one of six elevated tee positions, the fairway looks like trying to find a needle in a haystack! The top two tees are perched on the main coastal dune ridge and afford spectacular views across the course, and of the North Sea. However, from this elevated tee position you are visually deceived into taking on too much of the dogleg as the landing area appears wider than it is. From the other tees—set at a slightly lower elevation—although still higher than the landing area—one cannot really see the full magnitude of potential danger. Offering some respite, the angle of the fairway is, however, more favourable. A fairway bunker on the left denotes the dogleg point of the hole, and it serves as a guide for most players to aim at. However, unpredictable bounces often mean that a good drive—looking fairway-bound—can result in a hack out sideways from the awkwardly shaped fairway bunker. One gets accustomed to the scenario.

The better player may risk cutting off more of the dogleg by attempting a longer carry over the heavily vegetated sand dunes. Successfully achieved, the reward is another landing zone behind the bunker with a gathering area of reasonably flat land, and a good angle into the green. However, when the wind is directly into your face, this is no option to contemplate. Should the player decide against risking either of the above options, it leaves the way open for a deliberate tee-shot laid-up short of the bunker. The consequence of that is that the green will be out of reach for the second shot.

From short of the bunker, there is no easy lay-up option to the green; the fairway narrows, and the many humps and hollows ensure that any ball landing short of the green will end up in the rough. Worse still, it may catch one of the four gathering bunkers set within natural hollows to the edge of the fairway. This makes any kind of running approach very difficult, as the odds favouring an awkward bounce are high. However, even faced with a relatively short-iron to the green from the middle of the fairway, the aerial route of attack is not without some degree of unease. Thankfully, the green is elevated eight-to-ten yards above the fairway landing area, and slopes from back to front. And what a saving grace that is, being extremely difficult to stop even the softest balata golf ball on a sixpence when you have a breezy twenty-five miles per hour wind at your tail.

The green, itself, is a case of: 'don't be short, don't be long,' and once safely on its surface, you can expect an awkward putt. The ninth green slopes toward the middle from both sides and from back to front, so, consequently, no putt is straight, regardless of where the pin is located.

An unfair hole, perhaps? Not for me. Par, even birdie, can be achieved here ... but you'll need to exercise a lot of skill and have a certain degree of luck. In short: it is links golf in its purest form.

Harradine Golf
Dubai, United Arab Emirates

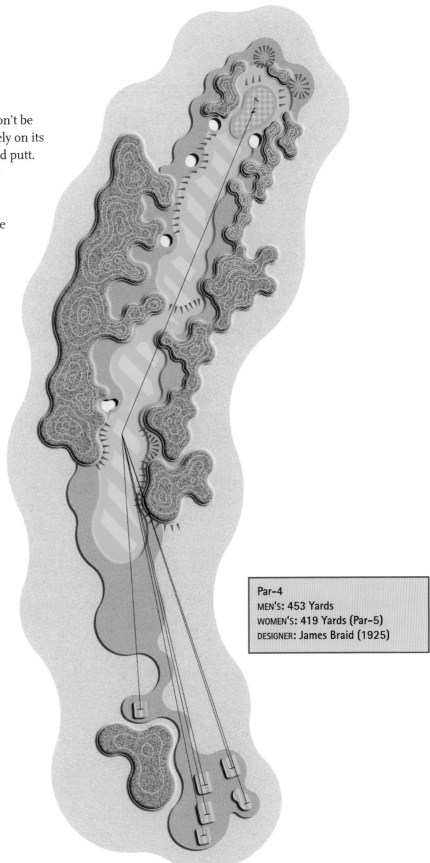

Par-4
MEN'S: **453 Yards**
WOMEN'S: **419 Yards (Par-5)**
DESIGNER: **James Braid (1925)**

The Golf Club at Cuscowilla, USA

Thirteenth hole Thomas Himmel

Golfers reserve the right to change their taste in what they like about a golf course, especially one that constantly changes. Their love of a single golf hole may also waver from time to time. This changeability may affect them on a favourite hole at their home course, or even apply to the most famous, spectacular and featured holes in golf.

When thinking about choosing my favourite hole, everything pointed to the par-four, thirteenth hole at Cuscowilla in Eatonton, Georgia. There may be more spectacular and famous golf holes that one could have chosen, but these have been fully and well elucidated over the years. This particular American hole has something very special about it. And yet, while sampling it for the first time, recognising the features is not straightforward; the hole is not well defined, in spite of it winding itself through large pine trees that are part of a former pine-tree plantation along Lake Oconee. I certainly don't intend to imply that the hole is not beautiful: it is that. Apart from a small amount of earthwork carried out upon the green and the various tees, no additional earthmoving was done to the fairway.

Doglegging slightly to the left, the hole runs impressively between the stands of pine trees. Those trees are so positioned that it calls for precise play, while the hole is still fair and playable by the average golfer. The thirteenth hole is without bunkers, and has a green where its front, left side, and part of the rear edges of the putting surface, slope into the surrounding fairway. The green sits so naturally within the existing topography that you can only just recognise the flag, and the brighter colour of the putting surface. In addition to the need for a right-to-left tee-shot, the approach to the green needs to be well struck and cleverly placed if the player wants to be rewarded with a holeable putt. As the putting surface itself slopes gently from right to left—approximately six inches over twenty-five feet—any ball curving slightly to the left will trickle off the putting surface, even when it has landed on the green. A 'bail' out to the right of the green, meanwhile, will leave a very tricky chip, pitch, or putt, from off the putting surface. The surrounds of the entire green are cut to fairway height, giving you all the desired options for the short game.

For good players, the strategy of the hole is to position the tee-shot moving gently left, into the dogleg. Gaining the optimum amount of curve will result in your ball taking advantage of a gentle and diagonal slope within the fairway. This takes effect at about 250 yards off the tee. Rifling the ball straight down the middle of the fairway represents good form on most holes. At Cuscowilla's thirteenth, however, it results in the player's second shot being blocked out by the group of pine trees on the right edge of the fairway at about 270 yards of the tee. The left-hand side of the fairway is protected by pine trees that under most circumstances cannot be carried. However, if you can hit the ball some 280 yards in the air with a pre-determined launch angle, plus have it reach the necessary altitude, the near impossible might just be achievable. But be warned: the slightest pull to the left when 'flirting' with the edge of these pine trees will end up with your ball being caught by the trees. The reward for a perfectly planned and executed tee-shot is immediate. Obviously, not all golfers are sufficiently gifted to orchestrate a deliberate right-to-left shot pattern. For these golfers, a reasonable option is to lay-up from the tee with a fairway-metal. This strategy will keep the right-hand group of trees out of play, but will leave a considerably longer approach shot to the green. This is fine: it may well be that a stress-free bogey five is all they seek.

Apart from the hole's great strategy and shot-values, I find it is the simplicity within its surrounding environment that makes the hole so appealing. It looks so harmless, and easy to play! Great credit must go to its designers, Bill Coore and Ben Crenshaw, for the harmonious and peaceful appearance that they have helped materialise.

Cuscowilla was opened for play in 1998, and when comparing it to most of the contemporary design work and shaping of golf courses, the thirteenth hole is so simple and designed so perfectly with what looks so little effort. For these reasons, I see greatness in it.

As a golf-course architect, I often find it somehow difficult—painful even—to do as little as possible and still create something exceptional. In this case, with the help of the outstanding topography and the existing environment, I believe this target has been perfectly achieved.

Thomas Himmel
Golfplatzarchitektur
Puchheim, Germany

CUSCOWILLA GC   HOLE 13

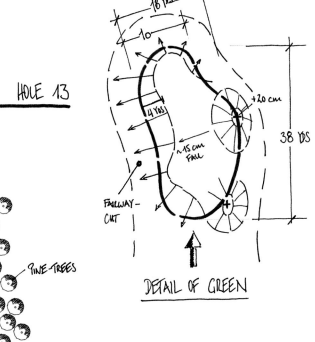

DETAIL OF GREEN

GREEN

PINE-TREES

STRATEGIC GROUP OF PINE-TREES
THAT ARE CRUCIAL TO THE HOLE.
(DISTANCE FROM TEE = 270 YDS)

STRATEGIC PINE-TREE THAT
HANGS INTO THE CORNER OF
THE FAIRWAY.

TEES

Par-4
MEN'S: 466 Yards
WOMEN'S: 372 Yards
DESIGNERS: Bill Coore and Ben Crenshaw (1998)

The Royal Melbourne Golf Club, Australia

Sixth hole: West Course Paul Daley

A golf hole with all the 'trimmings' can sometimes camouflage a forgettable design, yet holes do exist—seemingly drab—that fairly bristle with sound design principles. Yet, another scenario encapsulates Royal Melbourne's sixth hole on the West Course: exciting for golfers of all abilities to play; a highly relevant playing challenge; visually striking.

First-time visitors to the sixth tee must deal with an impressive and intimidating sight—a long band of heath, verging on 200 metres—stretching away down the right-hand side of the hole. Like moths drawn to the flame, it captures many tee-shots. Recognising the heritage value of such flora, a club sub-committee undertakes to preserve it, along with the many rare species of wildflowers throughout the thirty-six-hole complex. While the rough and sand dominate your eye-line, there is a vast fairway to the left of this, so most golfers needn't concern themselves with safe clearance. The shortest tee-shot carry is just under 200 metres, while it is progressively longer the further one drives to the right—an enticing option for top-flight golfers who seek an advantageous fairway position.

When viewing Alister Mackenzie's 1926 plan—prepared by Alex Russell—it's easy to see how he envisaged the sixth hole would be played. The first half of the golfer's journey heads broadly west, before turning northward toward the green. A solid line indicates the Scratch golfer's tee-shot line, and it traverses the heath. Another solid line denotes this player reaching the green—on in two—surely too easy? But as the plan was mapped out in the hickory-shaft era, such a carry over the heath could never be considered automatic, or risk-free. To illustrate the shorter hitter's strategy, a broken line is drawn well to the left of the heath, and then another punctuation signifies the ball coming to rest at the bottom of the hill, perhaps eighty or so metres from the green.

The Royal Melbourne layout opened in 1931, and Mackenzie's plan listed the sixth hole as a bogey five of 427 yards (389 metres). A significant change took place in 1936 when a massive bunker complex—the hole's prime feature today—was added to fortify the already-present heath along the fairway's right-hand side. The timing of this addition is worthy of deliberation: Mackenzie died in 1934, could such a monumental design element have been contemplated while he was still alive? Did the idea come to the wise men of Royal Melbourne—Alex Russell and Mick Morcom—during the two years following the master architect's passing, or had they years earlier envisaged the hole with these bunkers in place? Many would love to know. Prior to the 1936 bunker innovation, the hole's fairway hazards consisted of large bunkers that occupied 'high' ground on the outside of the dogleg. Although majestic in appearance, filling them in greatly improved the hole. Indeed, the sixth became more 'heroic' as a result, fulfilling a textbook description of the term.

By 1941, the hole had increased in length to 431 yards (392 metres), as golf ushered in the steel-shafted era. Around this time, golfers enjoyed an unimpaired view of the green from the tee, but this vanished following the planting of trees well past the inside corner of the dogleg. Prodigious hitting has never been the sole preserve of the contemporary golfer—prior to tree-planting the sixth hole had been driven on several occasions. An early Club Professional named Alex Orr was one of the more notable to achieve the feat.

When Melbourne's south-easterly wind is present, the sixth plays downwind and at its easiest. A medium-length hitter needs to consider adjusting their tee-shot line, perhaps being more adventurous than usual and biting off some of the dogleg. A long-hitter can easily run through the fairway unless their tee-shot is shaped from left to right. But when facing a northerly wind—even a gentle one—the diagonally placed bunkers must be given a wide berth from the tee. Relatively speaking, it is the powerful-hitting golfer who is most adversely affected by the northerly. Human nature being what it is, one's inclination is to not so easily surrender the 'bold' line, and so one is more likely to misjudge the wind strength and come unstuck. During professional tournaments when the south-easterly is in force, the field must at least contemplate usage of a three-metal in preference to a driver.

To return a decent score at Royal Melbourne, it is crucial on many holes to leave your approach shots below the hole. However, when the pin is situated in the front, left-hand portion of the West's sixth green—barely past a gaping bunker—doing so is fanciful. In the final round of the 2004 Heineken Classic, Ernie Els came to this hole at twenty-one under par with the tournament virtually

Par-4
MEN'S: 391 Metres
WOMEN'S: 337 Metres
DESIGNER: Alister Mackenzie (1926)

locked up. Mindful of the problems associated with coming up short, he played long; but it was too long, instead, finding the back bunker. The situation was tantalising: by attempting to get his ball close it would surely run through to the bunker in front of the green; by aiming left of the pin he would surrender any likely chance of par. Ernie aimed left of the pin, but splashed out too strongly. The gallery gasped as his ball trickled down the green, over the keenly shaven fringe, then back down the fairway. The Big Easy doesn't give much away, but he may well have been shell-shocked after his pitch back up the rise nudged to within three metres of the flag before temporarily ceasing, then rolling all the way back to his feet. The fiasco is commonplace during the Club's Medal rounds, but here was a golfing hero being made to look fallible—pencilling in a triple-bogey seven. The tournament came alive. Els eventually steadied to return a flawless inward nine of thirty-two, defeating

Adam Scott by one stroke to claim his third straight Heineken Classic.

A landmark change took place at Royal Melbourne around the turn of the last millennium when its greens were re-sown with Sutton's Mix grass. As a result, this green—once Royal Melbourne's most treacherous—is now a less nerve-wracking affair, although it can still produce humiliating putting experiences for careless, or overly confident golfers.

When compiling this book, I could scarcely believe my luck when one contributor after another nominated a wide range of favourite holes from around the world, and this superb hole had not been selected. It just goes to demonstrate one golfing truth: a golfer's favourite hole is intensely personal.

Full Swing Golf Services Pty Ltd
Glen Waverley, Victoria, Australia

MICHAEL COCKING '04

Augusta National Golf Club, USA
Twelfth hole Hisamitsu Ohnishi

Augusta National's twelfth hole, 'Golden Bell', holds a special place in my heart. When the 1990 Flower Expo was held in Osaka, the organisers came up with the idea of displaying this hole; as producer of the event, I negotiated with Augusta National and created a replica of this hole.

In the Expo, a hole-in-one contest was held for a period of six months, attracting golfers from all over Japan to try their luck. Each contestant was allowed just one shot, but only those who found the green putted out. The event drew a huge crowd, and, pleasingly, three holes-in-one were recorded.

Augusta's Golden Bell is a short par-three of 155 yards. However, this hole is so tough that even Jack Nicklaus once remarked: 'I aim at the centre of the green no matter where the pin is placed.'

With the twelfth hole lying at the lowest point of the property, it makes judging the swirling Amen Corner wind a most difficult task, which explains why so many tournament professionals refer to club selection as 'total guesswork.' And since the hole calls for a short-iron to hold the green, high trajectory shots are particularly affected by the wind. A further complication: the creek fronting the green is angled so that it catches tee-shots that are cut or sliced. Hence, many right-handed golfers tend to prefer hitting a strong draw.

One day during the Expo, Japanese golf star Naomichi Ozaki visited our pavillion, and he had just returned from playing in the 1990 Masters. Although the rule was just one shot per person, an exception was made to allow Ozaki ten shots as a TV camera was on hand to capture his shotmaking. However, he had difficulty making the green. I suggested that he play a left-to-right fade, rather than his draw, but he replied that it was difficult to assume a fade stance on this hole. But I insisted. He then changed from an eight-iron to a seven-iron and tried the fade. He caught the green beautifully. Since the green is designed so that the left side is closer, while the right side is further away—and only ten yards deep—draw shots are likely to land behind the left side of the green.

The 2003 Masters was won by the left-handed Canadian golfer, Mike Weir. With the flagstick in its customary Sunday position—far-right-hand portion of the green—Weir took aim well left of the flag, and then pushed it badly. Badly, is perhaps a misnomer: anything on this green is very good, and, at times, excellent! Over the years many fourth-round contenders have come to grief here, so Weir's par, courtesy of a gut-wrenching clutch putt, did him no harm. Meanwhile, his playing partner, Jeff Maggert, experienced first hand just what terrors Golden Bell has in store—twice visiting Rae's Creek—ending all possibility of victory. That he rallied late in his round with a succession of birdies showed us much about his determination.

Today's professionals hit the ball so much longer than those of previous generations. Their long-iron usage is usually confined to second shots into par-fives, or long par-threes over 200 yards in length. One senses that this is why so many contemporary architects design long par-threes. I personally believe, however, that par-threes should be short and tough, just like Augusta's Golden Bell. In fact, it's a hole that I always refer to as my 'Bible' when designing a course. This Amen Corner hole terrifies tournament contenders and will continue to produce dramatic events in the years to come.

Target Partners International
Tokyo, Japan

'Golden Bell'
Par-3
MEN'S: 155 Yards
DESIGNER: Alister Mackenzie and
Robert Tyre Jones Jr. (1931)

Ballybunion Golf Club, Ireland
Eleventh hole: Old Course Dr Michael J. Hurdzan

The eleventh hole at Ballybunion Old is one of those magical and unforgettable holes, the type that enchants golfers immediately. It certainly did with me. Most holes don't do that, so I have thought extensively about how it achieves that, and what makes this Irish hole so great.

The hole is a long but downhill par-four, ranging in yardage from 453 down to 385 depending on which of three sets of tees is being used. Since the entire right side of the golf hole borders the Atlantic Ocean at the mouth of the Shannon River, wind is always a factor and it is usually a right-to-left crosswind. You may say: thank heavens for small mercy! The basic strategy of the hole is to allow for the wind and strong left-to-right slope of the fairway, and place the tee-shot in the right half of the fairway before a series of terraces falling toward the green. However, guarding the right-hand side landing area is a reasonably deep hollow of rough fescue grasses—not a place from which you want to play a second shot. Following a perfectly placed drive, the approach shot is again downhill between two high dune complexes that are only a few yards apart, to a large green surrounded by fairway height chipping areas. Any mishit tee-shot, or one that doesn't properly allow for the wind and bounce and roll off the fairway, may well leave a blind second shot over the dunes. I find that such a shot is disconcerting enough, alone, to test the confidence in my swing, but when the green is perhaps fifteen to twenty feet lower than the fairway, it means making another mental adjustment in club selection. The green is also exposed to the full fury of the wind; not only must the wind be calculated for the last part of the approach shot, it is a common occurrence to allow for it while putting.

The view from the tee clearly reveals the hole's challenge and hazards, and the length of Ballybunion's eleventh hole is enough to require and reward a drive that is far and sure. Any tentative or miscued tee-shot amplifies the demand for a perfectly struck second: anything less can signal a bogey, or far worse.

Visually, the hole seems to be in perfect scale and balance. From the tee looking downhill to the wide fairway, the hole narrows through the gap in the dunes and culminates at a perfectly positioned green. Look no further than this hole to study a textbook example of single-point perspective. But, then, the view behind the green explodes into a seemingly endless succession of dunes, golf, water, clouds, and sky—elements that brilliantly frame the hole yet visually distort the distances and makes the scene almost ethereal.

This splendid display of golf-course architecture involves all of our five survival senses, and thus leaves a full and indelible experience burned into our memories. On the tee, and thereafter, your eyes seem to be constantly scanning the golf hole and surrounding area, for it is too large and too interesting to be fixated upon a solitary point of interest. Then there are the continually changing patterns of light and shadow as County Kerry's clouds sweep through. Serene harmony one moment: sheer turbulence the next! The sounds of the wind and waves fill your ears, punctuated perhaps by people, dogs or birds on the beach below. The smell and taste of sea air is inescapable, and the sense of touch is stimulated by the wind on one's face and the firmness of the ground beneath your feet. It is sensory immersion at its best.

Worthy candidates abound for any architect's favourite hole, but these reasons—and perhaps a few told over a cold beer—are why the eleventh hole at Ballybunion Old is mine.

Hurdzan: Fry
Columbus, Ohio, USA

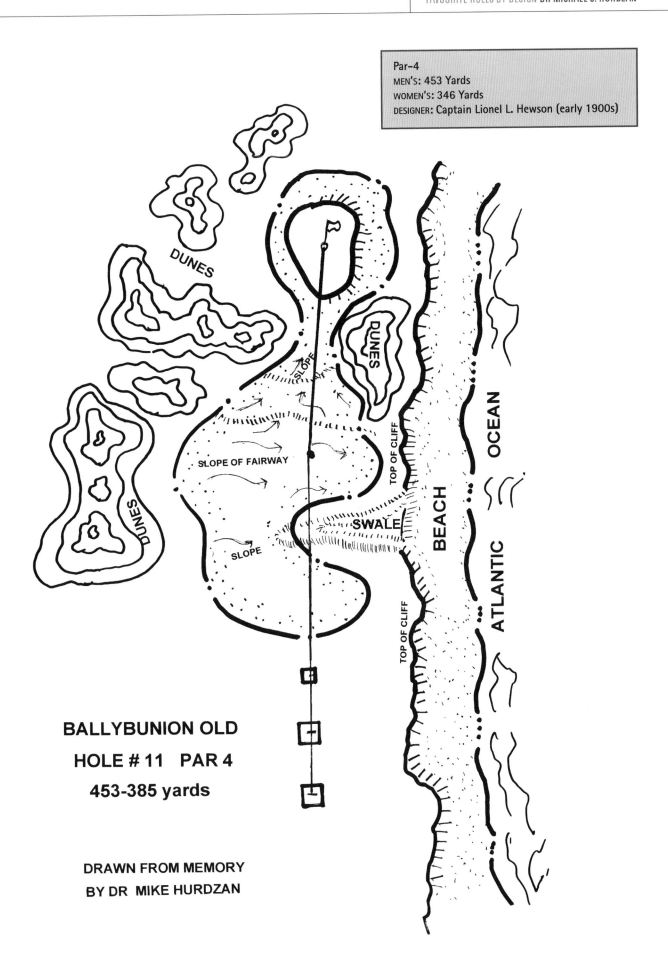

Par–4
MEN'S: 453 Yards
WOMEN'S: 346 Yards
DESIGNER: Captain Lionel L. Hewson (early 1900s)

DUNES

DUNES

SLOPE

SLOPE OF FAIRWAY

SLOPE

DUNES

TOP OF CLIFF

SWALE

TOP OF CLIFF

BEACH

ATLANTIC

OCEAN

TOP OF CLIFF

BALLYBUNION OLD

HOLE # 11   PAR 4

453-385 yards

DRAWN FROM MEMORY
BY DR MIKE HURDZAN

Ballybunion Golf Club (Old): Eleventh hole, Ireland.
(Photo by David Scaletti.)

The Royal Melbourne Golf Club, Australia

Fourth hole: West Course Michael Wolveridge

If ever there was a hole deserving of occupying the mantle: 'The Ideal Golf Hole,' then Royal Melbourne's West Course fourth—famously interchangeable as a par-four and -five—fits the bill. Designed from site during his historic visit to Australia in 1926, Alister Mackenzie, the grand master of golf-course architecture, along with his new acolyte, club champion Alex Russell, viewed the highest point on the course and ordered the surrounding area to be committed to a cluster of fierce, cavernous bunkers. Seventy-eight years later, the thought of entrapment still teases and taunts the majority of golfers standing meekly on the tee below, some 200 metres away.

Typically, there is an alternative way around the hazard, albeit, making the hole longer, and across a slope, which takes the ball further from the target with every bound. A safer play maybe, but rendering any hope of reaching the green with the second shot, remote, if not impossible.

I realised many moons ago that golfers of all skill levels, really do love the prospect of hitting over hazards. The universal law of golf has never altered: the more frightening the challenge, the greater the satisfaction one gains from successful clearance. We are, therefore, all hopelessly trapped somewhere between our commonsense, and our ego—that constantly recurring dilemma characterises the 'pleasurable excitement' of golf. Sand remains the most suitable hazard, leaving as it does, a sporting chance of successful escape. 'Water is so final, and has no place here,' so said Claude Crockford, revered curator of the East and West Courses for forty-five years, taking over his duties from the men who built them. Mackenzie, only too aware of the weaknesses of golfers, laid down the gauntlet on the fourth hole, beckoning us to take the bunker on and suffer the consequences of failure.

As I sat beside this famous tee musing to myself, on a breezy, summer's evening, I must have dozed-off as one does, for Tiger Woods and his caddie were chatting a few paces away, and the hillside above was lined with people as they awaited the great man's tee-shot decision. 'We'll take the two-iron Steve,' said the powerful American golfer. 'Mad,' I thought, asking myself why the stocky New Zealand caddie would

allow his charge to sidestep the challenge. But it was too late, he played his shot and the ball whistled away, sailing high above the awesome pit, still rising as the faces watching skyward followed his ball. It finally settled in the centre of the fairway on a slight downslope around 240 metres away.

Astounded and even affronted at the mockery of the iron, I watched as Tiger flashed his famous smile at me. It was clearly my shot! A driver appeared my best chance of a retort, and I teed up, knowing that the sympathetic support of the entire amateur golfing world was willing me across. 'I'll sort him out,' I muttered bravely and made a fair swing, just failing at the last gasp, as the collective groans told me that my ball lacked the required elevation to clear the bunkers. Walking slightly dejectedly up the steep hill, my mood nose-dived further when an observer stationed near the crest of the hill informed me of the extent of my near miss. He was holding his two hands perilously close—a sure sign that my ball hit the bunker's peak then, fell back into the sand. I approached my ball in the bunker. It was sitting well, but all I could see was sky. Mercifully, Tiger walked on past, and like the Pied Piper, dragged most of the spectators along with him down the fairway beyond the bunker. With no business at making such a mighty swing with an eight-iron, I made clean contact, sending the ball sky-high and out of the immediate danger. A modest cheer told me that my escape was successful. The shot felt pretty good, and the short sprint to the brow of the hill was exhilarating, as it always is in golf when you're the recipient of unexpected, good news. My ball came to rest on a gentle upslope, some fifty metres beyond Tiger's audacious two-iron from the tee.

The long and generous fourth green is located at the top of a rise, and is flanked on the left by a large bunker. The right-hand side of the green is strenuously guarded by a series of deep bunkers, fringed in true Royal Melbourne fashion by dense and attractive native plants.

There was still a breeze about—it is Royal Melbourne after all—and Tiger chose a six-iron for his second shot. I recalled how often I had watched Peter Thomson, the grand master of Royal Melbourne, preparing to squeeze the ball against firm turf with a long-iron from Tiger's

Par–5
MEN'S: 430 Metres
WOMEN'S: 368 Metres
DESIGNER: Alister Mackenzie (1926)

general vicinity, intent upon landing his ball between these bunkers then chasing onto the middle of the long green to set up his birdie four.

One feels certain that Mackenzie had this sort of golf in mind when he designed this splendid hole. It embraces the finest aspects of the game and sets the scene for a fair contest between master architect and champion golfer. For the rest of us mere mortals, a thrilling experience will have to do. Alas, the latest style of golf ball in the hands of the modern champion has rendered all such contests null and void. Great golf courses, worldwide, are now easily overwhelmed by the ridiculous performances that can be achieved by not necessarily tip-top golf. The creation of enormous length is out of all proportion to the level of skill required to combat carefully and skillfully designed playing fields. The current crisis in equipment technology has diluted the golfer's need for courage, expertise and experience. The game of golf is the loser, or is it?

As I glance across the fairway, Tiger is lining up his six-iron and aiming to land his ball by the flagstick, which is located dangerously close to a bunker along the right side of the green. My stocks are pretty low, for an eagle by Woods is entirely possible, and surely nothing worse than a four will follow. But there is just one glimmer of hope for an old stager: has Tiger fully accounted for the 'push' factor from his combination sidehill–downhill stance? I wonder. Goodness me: I'm done—he's knocked the stick out! But wait, the breeze and sloping lie take effect as his ball drifts ever so slightly to the right, ending in a greenside bunker. Tiger's ball has finished helplessly up against the bank, impossibly close to the overhanging native plants. There are times to ask for an autograph, but this is not one of them.

It's my shot. Remembering all the lessons at the feet of the earlier Masters, I gripped down on a seven-iron and prepared to 'coax' my ball onto the green. It was a good swing, nicely controlled—indeed, just like one of Kel Nagle's—my ball pitching short of the green between the bunkers and bouncing forward on the firm turf. It doesn't seem too special, but it's rolling, rolling, rolling on toward the centre of the green, and turning gently right as the power came off. Ten feet! And, as if it

was a daydream, to 'hearty' cheers. The rest is history, Tiger's ball was unplayable and I can't even remember if I needed to putt. I recall his lovely smile as I woke up beside the fourth tee, refreshed to do a piece on my favourite hole.

Michael Wolveridge
Melbourne, Victoria, Australia

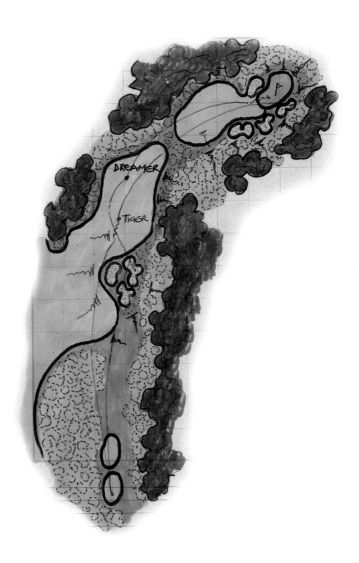

ABOVE AND OPPOSITE The Royal Melbourne Golf Club (West):
Fourth hole, Australia. (Photos by David Scaletti.)

Himalayan Golf Club, Nepal
Fourth hole Ronald W. Fream

The finest golf holes in the world, with a few exceptions, are those holes set unobtrusively into unique, natural landforms. There is great wisdom in exploiting the bounty of nature in the expression of distinctive golf. Evidence abounds that too many of the more recently designed courses give off the appearance of being plastic, forced, and contrived. Whenever this has occurred, only scant respect has been accorded to the natural environment. Too much rubber-stamping, or worse, flavour-of-the-month, ego-driven design is materialising. Moreover, golf maintenance has moved to the 'immaculate perfection' model typified by Augusta National in Georgia, USA.

Poles apart, there is Nepal: a golfing destination rarely considered and certainly not high on most 'must play' lists. Trekkers are far more aware of the significance of Nepal relative to Kathmandu, Mt. Everest, and the Annapurna massif.

To many people's surprise, golf does exist in Nepal. Luxuriant, sophisticated, and similar to golf in California, Florida, Korea, or Australia, it is not. Limited resources lead to limited results, even when local labour can be obtained to construct or maintain a golf course at wages of US$2 or $3 per day.

Himalayan Golf Club takes pride in its course forged by hand labour, to the design of a keen golfer, Major Ram B. Gurung. A Member of the British Empire, Gurung retired from the *British 2nd King Edward's Own Gurkha Rifles*, and acted upon a burning ambition to design a course to call his own. As an admission that land utilised as pasture for sheep, goats, and water buffalo on the outskirts of Pokhara was marginal, at best, it was obtained virtually free. Pokhara is the second city of Nepal and is the gateway to the majestic Annapurna Range of 8,000-metre mountains.

Ingeniously, Major Ram laid out eighteen holes within the seventy-five metre deep river gorge littered with the geologic debris of centuries of monsoon-induced water erosion coming directly south from the nearby Annapurna massif. Due to space limitations, several of the holes share fairways, or multiple tees. Whether it's for technical reasons, or persistence alone, this rough and rugged course is an extraordinary achievement.

The par-five, fourth and twelfth holes share a single greensite and fairway, but two diverse sets of tees. First time around, it measures 502 metres from the back-tee, while on the second rotation the hole is marginally shorter at 493 metres. The exciting tee-shot is across the Bijaypure River, which can either be a stream or a roaring torrent of turbulent water, depending upon the season. The entire riverbed, northward to an island greensite set within the river, is defined with exposed rock of varying sizes. The river's edge is comprised of landslide material from the Himalayan Mountains. Some of this material is smaller than the native sheep, but can also be larger than houses.

The elevated tee-shot has a diagonal target area, set among some exposed rock outcrops. And these rock outcroppings are substantial. When aiming one's drive across the river in an attempt to carry the first few outcroppings, one mustn't stray to the left. To help you picture the scene along the fairway's right-hand side, imagine a sheer vertical cliff-face rising in excess of seventy-five metres. Constant grazing by sheep, goats, and buffalo, has imprinted criss-crossing trails into the lower slopes of this cliff. Occasionally, the sheep or water buffalo are found grazing along the fairway. Consider the ongoing maintenance, and ensuing problems.

The fairway rolls and tumbles northward, while the cliff-face provides a backdrop for the entire length of the hole. Flowing water surrounds the rock-encircled, island greensite. When sizing up your second shot, options are reduced to two: lay-up short of water; or play with gusto toward the large, hybrid Bermuda green. Some may assume that in this harsh environment, a conventional green made from grass would be too big a luxury. But, pleasingly, there is no need to make do with oiled sand-greens.

Further adding to the hole's rustic look and unique character is, the northward view beyond the cliff wall backdrop. The village of Pokhara sits at 913 metres, while the fourth green is at approximately 838 metres. Looming bold and large beyond the green—and well in view for the second and third shots—stands the sharply angled mountain peak of Machhapuchare at 6,996 metres (22,952 feet). This glorious peak is also known as 'Fishtail.' Fishtail is not alone! Running east-to-west past this single pyramidal peak is the Annapurna massif. Annapurna I, Annapurna South, Annapurna III, and IV, can all be seen on clear days. Annapurna I hits 8,091 metres (26,545 feet) and Annapurna IV is 7,525 metres (24,688 feet). While playing, one does face depth perception challenges, and these stem from the visual distortion of the vertical walls of the deep river gorge, and that of the towering peaks beyond. Ravens circle overhead, while the gushing roar of the river remains constant. As a package, it is simply an inspirational setting.

Although the hand-pulled (three-manpower) greens mower keeps the Bermuda putting surfaces surprisingly smooth, you'll not encounter Augusta-like putting speeds at this altitude. As for the fairways, the sheep and water buffalo keep the Savannah-grass turf below shoe-top height. Play is best around the summer monsoon season—October to May—when temperatures are mild. The cliff-top clubhouse is basic, but the local beer is cold! Although the on-course views would surely satisfy anyone, golfers are gifted two additional views inside the clubhouse: Annapurna II at 7,937 metres (26,040 feet); and further to the east, Manasulu at 8,156 metres (26,758 feet). As there are only fourteen peaks in the world that rise above 8,000 metres, seeing two of them while playing the Himalayan layout makes it an unforgettable experience.

This course is every bit as rustic as Prestwick was, or St. Andrews, in the 1850s, emerging as they did from the raw fields of Scotland hundreds of years ago. The game in this form is truly organic: unadulterated and unspoilt golf. One quickly notices how the landscape is devoid of contrived course features. Come and see this 'unknown' treasure for yourself; you'll be proud of having ventured out of your comfort-zone to experience golf far removed from the urbane.

Golfplan—Fream & Dale Golf Course Architects
Santa Rosa, California, USA

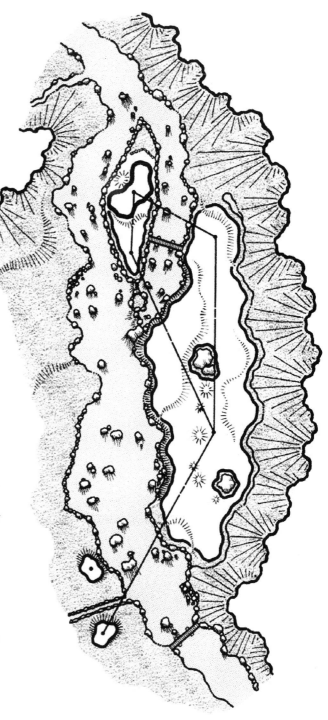

Par-5
MEN'S: 502 and 493 Metres
DESIGNER: Major Ram B. Gurung (1995-8)

Himalayan Golf Club:
Fourth hole, Nepal.
(Photos by Ronald
Fream, Golfplan.)

Kingsbarns Golf Links, Scotland
Sixth hole Brian Phillips

The greatest golf courses in the world usually have a number of world-class holes, and some of those may even be unique. Personally, I regard Kingsbarns as a world-class golf course. Perhaps some pundits would argue that it is overdone, and one occasionally hears snippets about it not being a true links. So be it, we all have opinions about such things. Okay, so Kingsbarns might not be the greatest test of golf, but surely it is more important for a golf course to provide an enjoyable playing experience to its customers. Nearly everyone agrees that Kingsbarns is tremendous fun to play, and that is a critical element, for the weather is not always too crash hot in Fife.

Unabashedly, I say that Kyle Phillips has designed a wonderful course. Together, he and his remarkable team produced a layout where the enjoyment level never lets up. Great and innovative holes were created at Kingsbarns by introducing the design element of liberal fairway width. The brainstrust must also have been mindful of presenting inter-hole variety for the three different par-types. By placing an emphasis on 'width' in the design of a hole, you automatically create playing options for a range of golfers' abilities, and that is why I have come to love the par-four, sixth hole at Kingsbarns. Combined with its width, a key factor is the length of the hole—it is within the yardage range where the good player can get confused on the tee, between knowing what they can do, should do, and would like to do.

The teeing ground is elevated above the fairway, which is divided into split-level sections and separated by two perfectly placed bunkers. The green is long and it slopes away from the line of play. As you stand on the tee there are several options at hand, and a definite decision on strategy will need to be made. This particularly applies to long-hitters. For instance: if you dare to take on the bunkers and successfully reach the higher part of the fairway, you'll be rewarded with a view of the green. If you are timid or a short-hitter, you can land your ball on the lower level of the fairway avoiding the bunkers, but this leaves only a view of the top of the flagstick. Should you be a powerful golfer then you can try to drive the green, but Phillips has conjured up a clever green complex that can be fun for the high-handicap player, yet also frustrating for the good player. The green slopes away from the play, and its entrance is quite tight if targetted with the drive. A pot-bunker awaits any drive, or approach, that is slightly off centre to the right.

So given all the golf holes that I've sampled around the globe, why should the sixth at Kingsbarns be my favourite? Well, I love matchplay—possibly because I am not a steady player—and this hole is a fantastic matchplay hole regardless of the weather. In a fourball, most players can make a par or birdie if they are courageous within their golfing ability, without having to rely on length as a factor. I appreciate the options that Phillips has provided—not only on the tee, but also from the fairway. When approaching the green, one has to decide upon the best short-game strategy: a bump-and-run into the green; or a high pitch-shot to try to hold the green? And, of course, there is another realistic option: to putt from forty yards out. Naturally, many golfers shy away from this option.

The sixth hole at Kingsbarns is the type of hole designed to introduce the lighter side of golf: to have fun while playing. Even so, some will depart the green with their egos battered and bruised. You stand on the tee with your stroke-saver in hand and you

<table>
<tr><td>Par-4
MEN'S: 337 Yards
WOMEN'S: 241 Yards
DESIGNER: Kyle Phillips (1997)</td></tr>
</table>

internalise that a birdie is manageable and not overly greedy. Invariably, though, you end up walking away muttering to yourself in the wind and pondering what went wrong. After close analysis of the hole, perhaps it's no real surprise that things don't often pan out for golfers. Afterall, the sixth hole presents all the elements that any golf-course architect would wish to design in a short, par-four, namely, the materialisation of both strategic and heroic features, and it even includes a penal element: the pot-bunker lurking beside the green.

It says much for the merit of this hole that, having just pencilled in an irritating bogey five, one doesn't hear of golfers being angered by it. And why? Because it was fun trying to outsmart the architect, and the hole! One may have failed dismally, but the fun was in the attempt. What more would a golfer wish for?

Niblick Golf Design AS
Moss, Norway

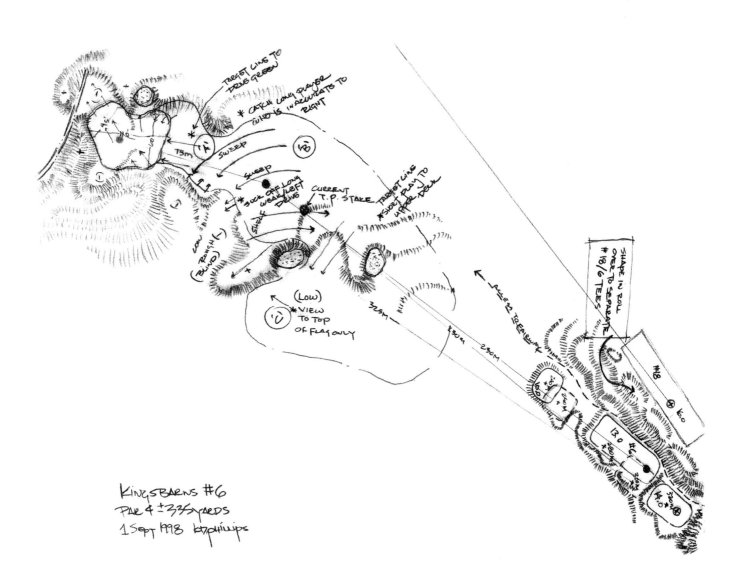

Kingsbarns #6
Par 4 ±335 yards
1 Sept 1998 kpphillips

Woodlands Golf Club, Australia
Fourth hole Graeme Grant

Woodlands Golf Club in Melbourne is blessed with a wonderful group of short par-fours, and, individually, each has withstood the onslaught of modern technology.

Stretched to a bare 251 metres in length, the fourth hole is the shortest of the group and can appear quite bland upon first sighting. Peering from the tee, one becomes aware of a lone bunker around 150 metres away, but this is well to the side, and it exerts little or no influence on the playing of the hole. A quick snap-shot: the ground slopes away and flattens out beyond the bunker; the boundary fence is positioned only five or six metres from the back of the green; and the eighth hole runs at ninety degrees behind the tee.

In laying out the course, it must have been a difficult proposition to fit the hole in the property. There would already have been enough par-threes, and this general vicinity may have appeared lacking in available space to cram in a par-four. But had the fourth hole not found its way into the final routing, Woodlands would have been less of a course today. Whichever way you dice it up, the green and its surrounds are the essence of the hole.

Given the nature of the ground, the restricted hole length, and other limitations, great imagination was the driving force behind the creation, and this has brought about a situation where the hole is so simple one day, yet so frustratingly complex the next. Although being a member of Woodlands for more than thirty years, I'm still somewhat perplexed at how such a short par-four with a fairway around thirty-five metres wide just short of the green can ever elicit any more than four strokes. Another intriguing fact: the more the members play it, the more they enthuse about its merit. So just how do we play it?

There are various methods, yet none are fail-proof. Each is capable of producing anything from a hole-in-one, to a double or triple-bogey.

When the hole is attacked with a driver, the long-hitter can easily attain a position of pin-high. In the modern era, that is no hand-clapping feat. However, the small, raised green is none too accepting: it tilts slightly from back to front, with a pronounced slope from left to right. The very narrow entrance

means that very few balls actually finish on the putting surface in one stroke. If the tee-shot is hit cleanly and gallops toward the green at speed, the odds are further reduced. Even when missing the green, one can be within eight or ten metres from the flagstick. In this instance, the upcoming chip shot is far from simple. The banks are very steep, with the green resting a little more than one and a half metres above the surrounds. And the target is alarmingly narrow. Rarely will one be afforded a straight shot up the bank; usually the shot will need to overcome an acute angle, requiring deft touch and local experience to 'nurse' the ball close. So often, though, I've seen chip shots finish right back at the player's feet. Not surprisingly, golfers are also mindful of not being too 'cute' with their chip. They then 'over-cook' the shot, and if it's only a whisker long, the ball seems to roll forever and eventually through to the other side.

From the tee, others may opt for a fairway-metal wood—a three or four wood in days of yore—or a long-iron, hoping to gain an angle of approach that is along the length of the green. One shouldn't assume that these golfers are lacking in boldness. Indeed, it may be simple case of having stored away some valuable knowledge from their previous round.

Any tee-shot that is headed just a little to the left, has a good chance of being deflected by the large mound twenty metres short on the green; this usually amounts to the ball bounding away onto firm, tight ground. The player must then decide whether to 'cut one up' to the green sloping away, or place their faith in a chip-and-run, which scurries up the bank. If the latter option is elected, two aspects will determine success: judging the speed; and the angle of deflection. From this location, however, an innocuous pin in the green's centre could be almost impossible to get your ball near.

If one cannot be straight off the tee, then a fraction to the right is marginally better; the tilt of the green helps to stop the pitch or chip. From a centre-right fairway position—even when really close to the green—the hole still throws up plenty of tricks. Everything revolves around your angle of approach, and the pin placement. A pin on the right-hand side seems to draw one too close to it, although it is known,

Par-4
MEN'S: 251 Metres
WOMEN'S: 241 Metres
DESIGNER: Mick Morcom (1931)

locally, that one should play well to the left to be sure of staying on. So often, though, the lure of making a birdie produces an overly aggressive chip that glides across the green and down the bank to the right.

A tee-shot that finishes excessively to the right, has the player trying to judge a lob-wedge across the narrow green from a lie that can easily cause a 'fluffed' shot. From this position—sitting tight on bare ground, or among tufts of indigenous grasses—a 'silky' touch and great skill is required to bring about a decent escape.

As the hole is so short, drives not infrequently scuttle on through the green. With trees to screen the boundary fence—ever so close to the green—nine times out of ten the player will find their ball in this scenario: 'dead as a doornail' behind the green.

Once on the green, the ridge feeding in five or six metres from the centre-back makes putting very interesting, especially when the pin is cut on either side. When you find your ball sitting on the wrong side of the ridge, a two-putt from as close as fifteen feet can be praiseworthy. Outside of this feature, the green is highly typical of Woodlands, where only modest slope near the hole is difficult to judge. Of course, all this 'build-up' is only for those who analyse and contemplate too much. Out on the course, and if one is on their game, the hole is quite simple: a tee-shot to the front edge of the green, followed by a decent chip-and-putt for a birdie three.

My reason for selecting this hole is that the golf architect and his team—to put it simply—'made something out of nothing.' In an era when earthmoving equipment was a horse and scoop, and so little earth could be moved, this was certainly the case!

Producing just the right degree of difficulty for a par-four of this length, and to have its features provide interest and excitement, even today, is the sign of an accomplished golf architect—maybe J. D. H. Scott from England, or, more likely, M. A. Morcom of Royal Melbourne fame.

Graeme Grant Golf Design
Melbourne, Victoria, Australia

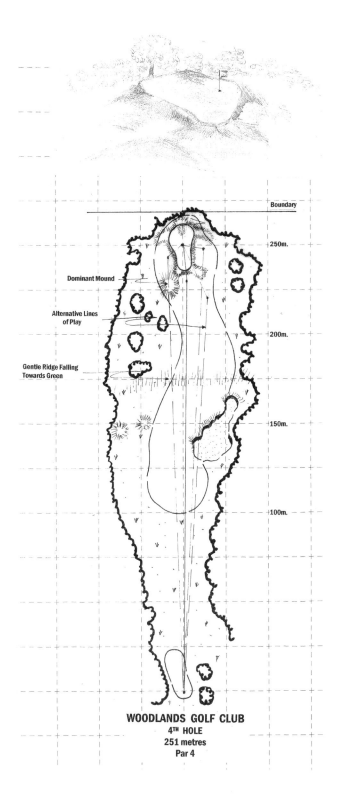

WOODLANDS GOLF CLUB
4TH HOLE
251 metres
Par 4

New South Wales Golf Club, Australia
Fourteenth hole Josh Taylor

Located on the northern headland of Botany Bay, the birthplace of Australia, sits one of the country's finest golf courses. As part of his whirlwind Australian tour of 1926, Alister Mackenzie was commissioned to revise the La Perouse layout—originally designed by Eric Apperly—on some of the most dramatic ocean-front property Sydney has to offer. With its undulating, sandy terrain covered with native Australian tea-tree tumbling down in a succession of ridges and valleys to a rugged, rocky coastline, the course is spectacular by any standard.

On paper, the par-four, fourteenth hole reads as a 323-metre hole that doglegs slightly to the left. But paper never quite presents the true picture, as the tee-shot view reflects a markedly different perspective. Here, even the strongest willed golfers will on occasion be distracted by the vista. There is a lot to take in as you ponder in awe at nature's perfection; you can't help but gaze out across the crashing waves of the Pacific Ocean, or even at the enormous cargo ships that glide their way into Botany Bay. Such distractions only add to the many nuances that make this hole a classic.

The angled tee-shot across a ridge; the saddled fairway; the elevated green that is exposed to the elements; a grassy hollow; and the thought of trouble awaiting any poorly executed shot, all contribute to the strategy of the hole. However, there is one more key factor behind its complexity: the ever-present wind—still the greatest defence against rampant technological advances. And not just any garden-variety wind—this NSW coastal wind can blow the dimples off a golf ball!

The wind is the most important factor in deciding how to play the hole. I have stood on the tee with driver in hand and mused over the possibility: 'I can knock this on the green,' but I've also experienced that unsettling feeling: 'I hope I catch this solid, or else I won't even clear that ridge'—a mere 190 metres away. The wind doesn't just wreak havoc with the tee-shot; it causes the approach shot to be devilish. An absolute must while preparing to drive is to accurately gauge the wind, then, trust your instinct; for upon reaching the seclusion of the saddled fairway, the wind does its darndest to fool you with its strength and direction.

One of the many tee-shot decisions you are forced to confront is the time-honoured classic: 'How much can I bite off,' and this is brought about by the angled tee-shot. But there are more aspects to consider than merely the line. The orientation of the green calls for an approach from the left, but only the boldest of tee shots in the calmest of conditions affords a simple pitch to this green. Any tee-shot that errs to the right will disappear out of sight and roll down to the bottom of the saddled fairway. Make certain you take the right club to assure that you finish at the bottom of the saddle; otherwise, you risk facing a lie with the ball well above, or below, your feet. And another prerequisite: be sure to hit the tee-shot solidly, or else you may not even carry the ridge and be left with a blind shot from an uphill lie.

Like all great strategic holes, the result of the tee-shot greatly affects the approach shot. Downwind, you don't want to be left too short a shot and unable to stop the ball on the firm, elevated green. When played into the wind, approach shots of any length to this tiny target surrounded by trouble are simply nightmarish. Your short game won't avoid being scrutinised either, for any shot that misses the green is faced with a delicate pitch. Should your ball go through the green, the rough-covered bank will cause you to wonder as you look at the slippery green racing away from you: 'Can I keep this ball on the green?' The grassy hollow short and right of the putting surface snares any miss-hit and the 'timid' at heart. Yet another aspect exaggerating the difficulty of the approach shot is the firm, playing conditions. From the tight New South Wales lies, there is no margin for error, and the wind accentuates any flaw in your strike.

No doubt you are starting to get the idea: there is a lot to think about when playing this hole. The hole has my total respect, for, seemingly, every day it throws up a different set of challenges depending on the wind. And doesn't golf need more holes like this: holes that mentally put you through the wringer, encourage considered shot selection, and then demand that you execute your shotmaking precisely. A seldom-mentioned quirk of this hole is the blind tee-shot and the

Par-4
MEN'S: **323 Metres**
WOMEN'S: **272 Metres**
DESIGNER: **Alister Mackenzie (1926)**

exhilaration that this gives players. When teeing-off, you're ignorant of the fate of your ball, and the next shot that will be required. That wonderful sense: the excited eagerness you feel climbing to the top of a ridge to see what kind of hand you have been dealt by the luck of the bounce, is too infrequently experienced in golf today.

The fourteenth hole at New South Wales has many desirable virtues: its setting is breathtaking; the natural undulations of the land are stunning; and, in the hands of one of the world's greatest golf-course architects, the result is, in my opinion, one of the most strategic and memorable holes to be found anywhere. Indeed, so

naturally perfect is the hole that the myriad of options presented to the golfer is created without a bunker. It is difficult to gauge which is better: the routing and design of the golf hole, or the fact that the architect appreciated what he had discovered and was able to restrain himself from imposing on the land in any way. In either case, both reveal the genius of Dr Alister Mackenzie, and, as such, the beauty and charm of New South Wales Golf Club.

Lehman Design Group
Scottsdale, Arizona, USA

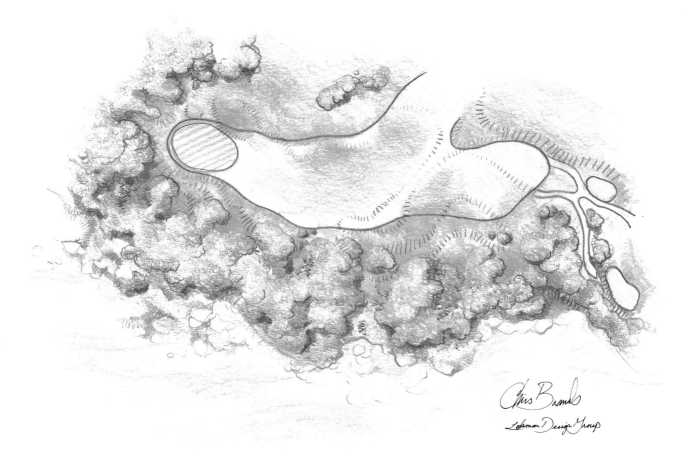

ABOVE Royal Dornoch Golf Club: Eighth hole, Scotland. (Photo by Larry Lambrecht, LC Lambrecht Photography.)

BELOW Royal Dornoch Golf Club: Fourteenth hole, Scotland. (Photo by Larry Lambrecht, LC Lambrecht Photography.)

OPPOSITE ABOVE Lahinch Golf Club: Fifth hole, Ireland. (Photo by Brett Mogg, Nelson & Haworth.)

OPPOSITE BELOW Ballybunion Golf Club (Cashen), Fifteenth hole, Ireland. (Photo by Brett Mogg, Nelson & Haworth.)

Crystal Downs Country Club: Sixth hole, USA.
(Photo by Larry Lambrecht, LC Lambrecht Photography.)

Gleneagles Hotel (Kings): Thirteenth hole, Scotland.
(Photo by Russell Kirk/GolfLinks Inc.)

St. George's Golf and Country Club, Canada
Second hole Thomas McBroom

Stanley Thompson's classic layout at St. George's Golf and Country Club has stood the test of time for seventy-six years, and is currently ranked as the top course in Canada. In common with all inspired designs, St. George's features eighteen intriguing and unforgettable golf holes. In 1928, Thompson walked the property's distinctive valleys and thickly wooded forests, and he enjoyed a most unusual opportunity. With over 2,000 acres of land at its disposal, the client—Canadian Pacific Railway—invited Thompson to choose the site to design and build this work of art for Toronto's new Royal York Hotel.

The fairways at St. George's are tree-lined and naturally rumpled. The combination of such stylish fairways, allied to subtly contoured greens, creates a sense of tradition and intimacy with the land that is unparalleled in Canadian golf. To decide upon a favourite golf hole is not an easy task; if there is one hole, however, that truly defines the character of Thompson's vision, and captures my imagination, it is the second at St. George's. In a highly unorthodox (for the period) yet brilliantly calculated manner, Thompson didn't merely route the holes through the fissured valleys; he utilised these steep-sloping landforms strategically to create brilliant golf holes, and what he achieved on the second hole is arguably his finest example. Traditionally, most valleys run parallel with the direction of the hole, but at St. George's, Thompson incorporated them to run both perpendicularly and diagonally to the flow of play.

In 2004, the course plays to a par of seventy-one and now stretches out to 7022 yards from the championship tees. From the forward tees, it is reduced to a 5,348-yard par of seventy-three. Today's course is several hundred yards longer than Thompson's original design, which is only to be expected given the passage of time.

The course commences with consecutive par-fours. The first hole is relatively short at 370 yards, playing from an elevated tee into a generous valley, then rising some seventeen feet to a beautifully shaped green: a welcoming warm-up to the player's round.

When standing on the second tee and peering down the tree-lined fairway to the distant flag, the prospect on first glance doesn't appear overly threatening. However, the scorecard tells a different story. At 466 yards from the championship tees, it is the longest of the nine par-fours, and plays as a par-five from the forward tees. This compelling golf hole requires two excellent, well-planned shots very early in the round. It's about strategy, as well as execution, and there's no other hole like it on the course.

The tee-shot calls for a strong drive from one elevation to another, over a dramatic valley, while carrying a rolling up-slope that runs from left to right, to the landing area some 250 yards away. Although the landing area is generous, Thompson's design places emphasis on powerful-hitting golfers shaping their tee-shots from right to left through the up-slope, to a level landing area. Assuming success, this sets the stage for a mid- to long-iron into a slightly raised green protected on both sides by bunkers and fall-aways. If the tee-shot veers too far to the right, it will usually finish in a semi 'blind' and awkward position—the contouring of the land also directs the ball toward the right-hand-side bunker. And once your ball is bunkered, the likelihood of par is greatly reduced because of the bunker's steep face and overhanging trees, which come into play.

Bordered by century-old oaks, the fairway narrows—alarmingly for the inaccurate or those inclined to 'steer'—for the approach shot to the green. Down the left-hand side, Out of bounds also comes into play. The ideal second shot will thread the needle between diagonally set bunkers to the final element of the hole: a long, narrow green sloping from back-to-front, plus left to right. Any time you find yourself above the hole, putting becomes downright perilous—take two-putts gleefully, and aim next outing to give your nerves a break by being under the hole.

Before exiting from the second green, you should take the opportunity of gazing back up the hole. You'll shake your head as you contemplate the genius that was Stanley Thompson. To my way of thinking, Thompson has captured the naturalness of this land and moulded St. George's routing into a visually compelling and strategically brilliant masterpiece—his greatest work!

Thomas McBroom Associates Ltd.
Toronto, Ontario, Canada

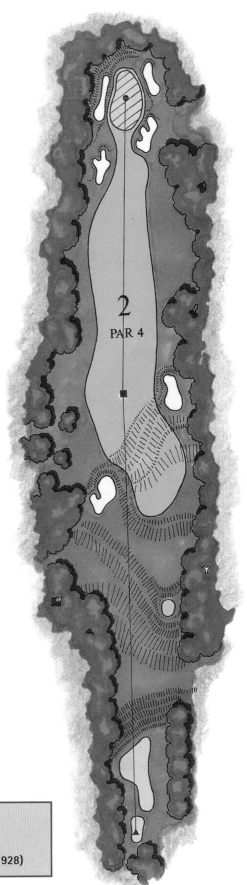

Par-4
MEN'S: **466 Yards**
WOMEN'S: **400 Yards (Par-5)**
DESIGNER: **Stanley Thompson (1928)**

The Royal Melbourne Golf Club, Australia
Third hole: East Course Peter Williams

Attempting to nominate my favourite golf hole is no easy matter, and while this decision is fraught, it is done so with admiration of the past great architects, namely, those from the Alister Mackenzie and Alex Russell era. And so I 'tip my hat' to the third hole on Royal Melbourne's East Course, designed by the latter designer, and weighing in at barely 350 metres. Over the recent past there has been a couple of variations from the traditional Royal Melbourne Composite Course routing. The par-four, third hole on the East Course is traditionally played as the fifteenth hole of that layout.

A favoured aspect of exceptional golf design is the subtleties contained within the great, short-to-medium length par-fours of the world. And Melbourne has some of the best! Such holes are often mentally taxing on the tee, exposing one's playing skill, accuracy, self-control, and putting. Interestingly, these holes can also test a golfers ability to hit precise distances in order to best take advantage of the terrain, particularly, to gain the best approach angle into the green.

Invariably, the sport of golf comes down to playing ability and tenacity, combined with deliberation and evaluation of design strategy, along with factoring in the environs. This is the intrigue, or scheme of golf design, and what makes for great golf. I am certain that golf-course architecture will never cease in the ongoing pursuit to harness the gambit of golf, drawing out and highlighting the talent of good golf. Such is the case with the third hole on the East Course.

While its teeing ground is significantly above the turn of the dogleg, it is virtually level with the fairway's left-hand side, giving rise to terrain falling diagonally from left to right toward the prized 'go' zone: the relatively flat base of the dogleg some 240 metres from the tee. Following precise play, this same terrain tends to propel tee-shots toward the fairway's base. When the great players descend upon Royal Melbourne at tournament time, one sees first-hand how important it is for superior playing skills to match the subtleties of the hole. Indeed, it is intriguing to see golf design, and the game, so worthily aligned and assessed.

The attractiveness of the 'incentive' zone at the turn of the dogleg is essentially a result of fairway and rough profiling. This design element—fairway meeting rough—is a result of golfing knowledge and astute, local crafting. Flora foliage does play a part in this golf hole, with penalties resulting from misdirected length through the centreline of the fairway, and also to its right-hand side.

Assessment of great golf holes and how they came to pass is without question vast, and often open to opinion. In the case of Royal Melbourne East's third hole, one could pose the question: is it the presence of an intriguing landform that sets up a highly advantageous, but narrow, 'incentive' zone, or is it the craft of design architecture? I am inclined to suggest the latter.

The flat turn of the dogleg provides 'incentive,' for straying both left and right with the tee-shot usually results in getting caught up on the diagonal decline. And then there is the lay of the land, which results in the ball resting either diagonally above, or below, the stance. Perhaps the greatest consideration with this tee-shot is deliberation over club selection, coupled with clever use of the landform, in order to obtain the desired fairway position.

As a green guarded heavily by bunkers, things are tight, but not in any claustrophobic manner. Bunkers appear front-right, with a reasonably detached right-side bunker, whereas, the left-side bunker abuts the green, with a detached bunker lurking several metres to the centre-rear, left of the green. The rear, left-hand bunker is several metres past the green, and some may aver that it has little strategic value. But to my way of thinking, this bunker demonstrates the skill of designers from the Golden Age of golf-course design. While nearly on a level plane with the green, there lies a slight swale between it, and the green, setting up what is commonly termed as 'dead' ground. From the fairway, players would swear the bunker abuts the green. Such a talent for visual subtlety in golf design reflects astuteness, design intent, and mental agility. Such visual strategy will always complement good design principles and impact upon play. While the bunkering etches into the character of this golf hole, it is the green's surface design that allows for truly exciting pin positions over the four days of tournaments.

Par-4
MEN'S: 350 Metres
WOMEN'S: 316 Metres
DESIGNER: Alex Russell (1930–31)

Many are inclined to think of the third East's green as a work of art. Pivotal to its design is a swale in the middle-right section. This extends to the green's centre, at which point, it separates the green into sectional areas designed to accommodate pin placement. When the pin is stationed in a front-right position, avoiding the over-hit and swale calls for accurate club selection, and fine judgment. Playing toward the front-left pin also calls for accurate play, as wayward golf finds the left bunker. Avoiding the decline toward the swale demands skilful bunker play. Both the left-rear side pin, to the middle-pin present difficulties for golfers, in that the pin is in proximity of the central apex to the swale, at which point the surface tilts slightly toward the rear left, and in line with play. The rear-right pin forms a plateau, albeit, one that it is not overly accentuated from the fairway. However, the swale bank—oblique to play—is impactful and demanding of accurate club selection, given the lack of target zone. Again, only credible play is rewarded.

We can take for granted the outstanding equipment available now, and today's power-hitting golfer never ceases to amaze, but when such talented and fortunate golfers find themselves in the midst of favourable wind and fairway conditions, the third hole becomes reachable in one prodigious stroke. While most would assume that such a scenario did not enter the strategy equation in its formation, I sense this is wrong, on account of the right, approach bunker being situated in a strategic position that offers protection against the attempt. In a genuine design balance between incentive, and entrapment, there is scope for credible play to reach the green in one shot.

The third hole on the East Course may demand deliberation and understanding of design in considering plays available. However, this hole, while seemingly harnessing length, fills the absolute need of patience and decisiveness. Can there be a conclusion, perhaps not, as the dynamic of the sport of golf and design strategy and architecture is about ongoing challenge and potential reward. Certainly this marvellous hole has a very high standing in the game of golf.

Peter Williams & Associates Golf Course Design/Services
Robina Woods, Queensland, Australia

National Golf Links of America, USA
Third hole Brian Schneider

With the possible exception of The Old Course at St. Andrews, my firm conviction is that there is more to be learned about golf architecture in the first six holes of Charles Blair Macdonald's strategic masterpiece—the National Golf Links of America—than in the full eighteen holes of any other golf course in the world.

The introduction to any course should leave an impression, and what glorious holes are housed within the first third of this incomparable journey. Commencing with the short, par-four first, the course announces itself with a variety of options from the tee, plus one of most severely contoured greens imaginable—surely among the game's finest openers. The 'blind' tee-shot on the drivable second hole, 'Sahara', is at once disconcerting and comfortable, exacting and thrilling. It is enough to say that the fourth hole is widely considered to be the finest example of a 'Redan' hole on the planet! Then there's the fifth hole, 'Hogs-back,' which includes dramatic cross-bunkering and ingenious use of natural contour as a driving hazard. And the sixth hole, known as 'Short', flies in the face of convention by utilising a massive and wildly contoured putting surface—in spite of being the shortest hole on the course.

In the midst of so much greatness and sporting excitement is the par-four, third hole: 'Alps'—the one I most look forward to reacquainting myself with when visiting the National. Macdonald gained his inspiration for this hole from the infamous seventeenth hole of the same name at Prestwick, Scotland. The existence of such a hole is not only testimony to Macdonald's vision and genius as a designer, but is also a reflection on just how much golf architecture has evolved since the course opened in 1909.

From a perch below the famed windmill—above the sheltered fairway—the view of 'Alps' is inspiring; one is instantly struck by the imposing scale of the hole, along with the unusual but stunning arrangement of its features.

For the tee-shot, golfers are at liberty to choose their preferred starting line, based upon one's confidence level in clearing some, or all, of a long, diagonally placed bunker that guards the front-right of the fairway. At the range of a good drive, the mammoth hill from which the hole takes its name begins to encroach from the far left-hand side of the fairway, forcing the long-hitter to adopt a more aggressive line up the fairway's right-hand side. With each yard that you venture to the right, visibility of the hole improves, though, you can never see as much as you'd like. From the fairway's right-hand side, golfers are faced with a daunting, long approach shot—completely blind over the bulk of the fescue-covered 'Alps'—with precious little to aid alignment.

A series of hidden bunkers traverse the line of play—some twenty yards short of the green—so that only a positive and well-struck approach shot will reach the putting surface. Additionally, the third green is protected along its right-hand side by a considerably deep bunker, and it features enough internal contour and right-to-left slope to make the act of two-putting from the 'wrong' side, a very worthy accomplishment.

For the player who decides—through good judgment, or lacking the courage of their convictions—to tackle 'Alps' as a three-shot hole, Macdonald provided an alternative route along the right-hand side of the hill, where the fairway continues to within fifty yards of the green. Golfers who elect to play the hole in this manner will still need to remain alert: a carefree bogey is not automatic. They'll still need to contend with a deep fairway bunker, and the cant of the elevated putting surface, which runs away from the shot. These elements provide plenty of interest and intrigue for those who choose this cautious route of play.

'Alps'
Par–4
MEN'S: 426 Yards
WOMEN'S: 378 Yards
DESIGNER: Charles Blair Macdonald (1909)

A patch of short grass sitting atop the 'Alps' provides yet another option for those playing 'safely' with their second shot. Although the crowned fairway remains mostly hidden, and is hard to hold, the short approach shot from this position is relatively straightforward and inviting. By presenting such an abundance of playing avenues, it has enabled the number one stroke-index hole to remain manageable and fascinating to every class of player.

The majestic 'Alps' embodies the characteristics that make the National such a special place: the grandeur and drama of the property; the wide array of alternative routes from tee to hole; the complexity and scale of Macdonald's bunkering schemes; and the massive, brilliantly conceived green complexes, which ensure play of endless interest and pleasure.

In the intervening period since the National was built nearly one hundred years ago, holes like 'Alps' have sadly gone out of favour with many golfers, and, subsequently, with course designers and developers as well. Yet these very same landmark holes, namely, 'Peconic,' 'Valley,' 'Punchbowl,' and 'Alps'—holes of character and charm, of quirk and whimsy—are precisely the reason why the National is the most rewarding course I've had the pleasure to study and play. It is a veritable textbook of golf architecture, and a true treasure of the game.

Renaissance Golf Design, Inc.
Traverse City, Michigan, USA

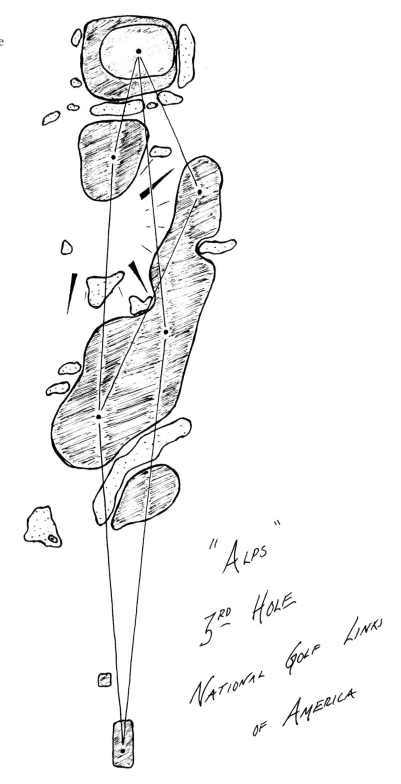

"Alps"
3RD HOLE
NATIONAL GOLF LINKS
OF AMERICA

Prestwick Golf Club, Scotland
Fifteenth hole Patrick J. Burton

Scotland is blessed with perhaps the best venues for links golf in the world. Undoubtedly, people rattle off St. Andrews, Muirfield, Carnoustie, Royal Troon, and Royal Dornoch in association with Scotland's best courses. Their bias toward the big-name links is understandable, but all too frequently golfers overlook Prestwick, my favourite links along the West Coast of Scotland.

Prestwick's credentials are beyond reproach, being the birthplace of the Open Championship in 1860, the one-time home of Old Tom Morris, and a links riddled with intricate internal course features. This early golf centre literally teems with history and nostalgia for the keen student of golf-course architecture.

Prestwick is laid out upon fiendish, unrelenting linksland: one of the most spectacular and undulating parcels of land I've encountered. Quirky is a tag it has long endured, but it may best describe the routing, which originally started out as twelve holes in the 1800s, and was later altered to an eighteen-hole layout.

Several of the most famous and fantastic holes in golf are found at Prestwick. In a flash, one recalls the third hole: 'Cardinal', featuring the Cardinal Bunker—one of the most notorious hazards in the game. There is the celebrated fifth hole: 'Himalayas'—a long, par-three requiring the golfer to aim at a small target on a hill, which must be carried, to a 'blind' green flanked by five bunkers. The green, by the way, isn't overly conducive to accepting shots. Love it or hate it, this hole simply cannot be ignored, and you'll need to get past it to keep your score intact. There's also the treacherous seventeenth hole: 'Alps'—a par-four requiring a 'blind' second shot, which has been duplicated many times on some of America's most prestigious courses.

Great as the above holes are, my favourite is the par-four, fifteenth hole: 'Narrows.' The Narrows might be one of the nastiest holes I've ever played. A daunting tone is set before you even reach the tee, knowing that you're about to play four of the most difficult finishing holes in Scotland. As you look toward the landing area you see thick, gnarly, knee-high rough on the right, and the same treatment on your left. Look again, and you may just catch a glimpse of a small piece of wicked, rippling terrain between these troublesome areas. Well: that's the elusive fairway! The tee-shot is visually intimidating, especially, the sight of four sod-revetted bunkers flanking the fairway's right-hand side, which to some degree protect errant shots from entering the dunes. But, cruelly, there is a fifth bunker 'blind' to golfers patrolling the left-hand side of the landing area. It's a shame this feature is only 190 yards or so off the tee now, making it almost a museum piece and easily carried by most players. Bear in mind, though, that golfers used to tackle this hole with a feathery ball and hickory shafts.

After the tee-shot has been conquered, and the odds would always be against that, securing a par is by no means sown-up. The slightly uphill approach shot is directed toward a green that is mostly 'blind.' Only the top of the flagstick is visible: a concept seen at many British links. To make matters more difficult, the fifteenth green slopes away from the golfer and falls away to the left, so even good shots don't automatically hold the putting surface. Putting is the easiest aspect of the hole, as the green boasts only modest undulations when compared to others at Prestwick. Maybe so, but when you're putting for a double-bogey six, or worse, this awesome hole can still manage to leave a sour taste in your mouth.

Forrest Richardson & Associates
Phoenix, Arizona, USA

'Narrows'
Par-4
MEN'S: 347 Yards
DESIGNER: Old Tom Morris (1851)

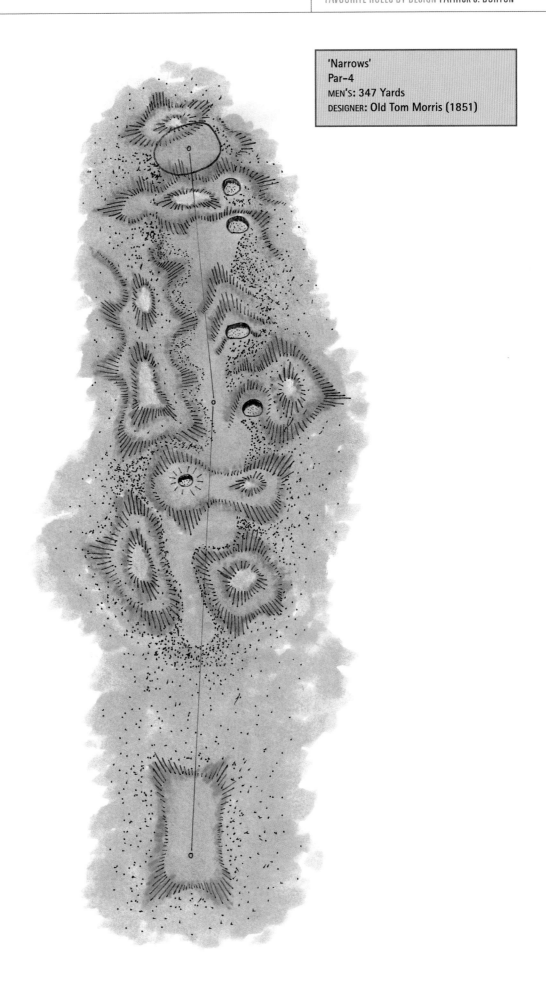

Moselem Springs Golf Club, USA
Tenth hole Kelly Blake Moran

Moselem Springs—a golf course in my hometown—was built in 1964 on the family farm of the publisher of the local newspaper. Hawley Quier, the owner, brought in golf architect George Fazio, whom exceeded Mr. Quier's expectations when the course was completed. A mere four years later, Moselem Springs hosted the 1968 Women's US Open Championship, and has since been the site of many prominent tournaments.

The tenth hole is especially fun to play because all of the shots from tee to green are highly anticipated. To put the hole in context—an uphill par-four of 397 yards doglegging to the left—you must examine the holes immediately before and after the tenth. On the holes prior to the tenth hole, it is necessary for golfers to shape their drives, but just slightly. However, starting on the tenth hole, and likewise for the following two holes, golfers must shape their tee-shots in a dramatic way to have any success.

The eighth hole is a long and mighty par-four that bends to the left; the ninth is a par-four that moves gently to the right, and one where a left-to-right tee-shot is logical, yet dangerous to play. Skipping ahead, the eleventh hole is a sharp, left-to-right par-four, while the twelfth is a sharp, right-to-left par-five. In sequence, from the eighth tee through the twelfth tee, the holes are designed right to left, left to right, right to left, left to right, and right to left. Clearly, George Fazio devised an excellent routing.

The tenth hole tee-shot is the first one on the layout requiring the better player who chooses a driver, to work the ball, or risk driving the ball into a bunker, or a dense forest of pines, on the outside of the fairway. What heightens the strategic design of the hole is the challenge and temptation posed by a menacing creek on the inside of the dogleg. Serpent-like, this creek enters at a point above the green to its right, winds in front of the green, cutting off the fairway from entering the green, then parallels the fairway down its left side then departing the hole to refresh a creek near the eighteenth green.

A better player can play a right-to-left tee-shot to a fairway that is angled to the line of the tee-shot. Hopefully, the ball will roll off the pronounced slope, and settle in the flat part of the fairway near the creek. Careless, and 'over-cooked' shots, can easily find the creek.

For some, there is another tee-shot strategy: to aim in the direction of the creek and attempt to carry it! This bold route—a more direct line at the green—will be rewarded with a much shorter approach shot. By attempting the long play over the creek, it provides an avenue for having the ball come to rest on the flat part of the fairway near the creek: position A! Attaining this fairway position is especially helpful when the pin is stationed on the right-hand side of the green. The real payoff is that you play toward the longest axis of the green, and you can play your favoured shot from a level stance.

Another tee-shot choice is to play on a direct line to the green, over the creek, and drift the tee-shot into the sloping fairway. No method will suit everybody, but this one does eliminate any chance of the ball rolling into the creek. The downside is that successful execution leaves the ball upon the sloping part of the fairway, making the stance more problematic for the approach shot.

Finally, some choose to play safe with a fairway metal from the tee—taking the bunker and trees out of play—and taking advantage of the fairway that is mostly flat in the area before the bunker. This option, however, leaves the player with an extremely long approach shot to the well-guarded green.

An average player who hits their drive 200 yards will be well short of the fairway bunker, but now must face an uphill approach shot measuring about 185 yards. About 140 yards into the flight of their approach shot, the ball encounters the creek that comes across the approach area to the green, so the ball must stay in the air probably another ten yards to clear the creek; it's another twenty-three yards to the front of the green once past the creek. In the approach area short of the green, there is a narrow, abrupt slope that ascends to the green. The narrow approach area is sandwiched by two bunkers that burrow into the slope. The approach area is low in the middle, and high on the edges near the bunkers. The wise player may want to play their second shot to a safe spot short of the creek, and then

Par–4
MEN'S: 397 Yards
WOMEN'S: 353 Yards
DESIGNER: George Fazio (1964)

rely on a pitch shot of around sixty yards to the green. Recording a five here is an excellent start to the incoming nine.

If safely on the fairway, the better player must seemingly only select the right club, then, execute the shot. But it is not that easy. Leaving aside two telling aspects—the greenside bunkering and narrow green—the player must first judge the effect of the elevation change up the hill from the fairway to the green. Irrespective of how often you play the hole, errors occur mainly by misjudging the distance: the uphill incline appears to be modest, and yet it is a long slope from the fairway up to the green. Additionally, the distance from the edge of the creek to the green is much greater than what you imagine. In spite of the modern conveniences at your disposal to ascertain the right distance, one is still inclined to underestimate the uphill climb to the green. It happens all the time.

The tenth green at Moselem Springs is oval-shaped, with its high point on the back, right-edge of the green. Much of its surface is visible from the fairway, except for the right-hand portion with its guarding bunker. The surface descends toward the front left-hand bunker at a rate of around three per cent, so any putt from above the hole can be downright treacherous. The middle portion of the green is a swale; most putts break appreciably, and do so quickly.

Hopefully, I've managed to translate just how exciting this hole is to play, and outline the twists and turns that may occur depending upon the decision at the tee, and the decision on the approach shots from the fairway, or the rough. While reflecting upon the day's play in the clubhouse, many golfers ruefully recall their decision-making on the tenth hole, shaking their heads at how it changed the course of the match.

Kelly Blake Moran Golf Course Architects, Inc.
West Reading, Pennsylvania, USA

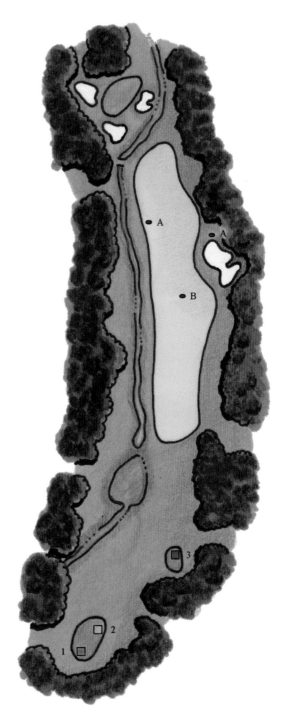

TEE	POINT A	POINT B
1	260 yards	
2		200 yards
3		160 yards

Palm Meadows Golf Course, Australia
Eighteenth hole Graham Papworth

The finishing hole at Palm Meadows on the Queensland Gold Coast is one of the most dramatic strategic/heroic holes in Australia. Quite unashamedly, this very well designed hole displays the risk-and-reward principles that strategic golf design is all about.

A heroic hole can also be viewed as strategic: when it provides alternative lines of play for the less proficient player to complete the hole—albeit, taking a shot or two more than if one successfully adopts the heroic line.

The par-five, eighteenth at Palm Meadows epitomises such conditions of play from tee to green, and the line for every shot depends on how confident you are with your distance and striking ability.

During the Palm Meadows Cup, played from 1988 through to 1993, the hole was always the scene of much high drama. Offering so many potential results—from a possible eagle three, to a devastating fifteen taken by one professional in his round of eighty-one at the 1990 Cup—participants and spectators alike found themselves in a heightened state of expectancy.

Being the richest golf tournament in Australia at the time, the Palm Meadows Cup was eagerly awaited by the Gold Coast's golfing fraternity who appreciated watching the play of many of the world's best international players, coupled with the best local and national golfers.

Invariably, the eighteenth hole provided the possibility of a major turnaround, and the final round of the 1990 event was a case in point. Playing in the final group, Curtis Strange—winner of the 1989 Cup—was one shot ahead of his playing partner, Rodger Davis, when they came to the last tee. Playing first and with everything to gain, Davis carried the corner of the massive lake, creating the opportunity to reach the green in two shots. Strange played the hole as he had done all week, opting for a conservative tee-shot line well left of the water.

Rodger finished with birdie to Curtis's par, and a play-off was called for. After both players secured their par-threes on the seventeenth hole, it was back to the eighteenth tee. This time, given the added pressure, Davis's carry over water was even more impressive, landing well beyond the palm trees as shown on the accompanying sketch. But it was Rodger's second shot—also a water carry to the green—that was even more impressive, finishing about six feet from the pin. This audacious display of shotmaking set up an eagle and a famous victory.

The real beauty of the hole is that the playing decisions and degree of satisfaction gained from achieving your shot are just as satisfying for the 'C' grade player, as they are for the tournament professional, as well as for those of varying abilities in between. No matter what shape your game is in, the pressure doesn't let up. Even playing safe requires accurate play and steady nerves.

In addition to the compulsory water carry in front of the green, there is a collection of hazards around it, including a ball-devouring clump of bamboo—one of the few natural features remaining from the original flood-plain site.

Although the green slopes toward the golfer and is generally receptive, the slope is sufficiently severe to put the onus on getting your ball close, and preferably below the pin. Naturally, this places more emphasis, and pressure, on the water carry when the flag is positioned well forward.

The eighteenth hole at Palm Meadows provides a terrific finish to a round, and can destroy a great seventeen-hole score so very easily. However, if played successfully, and to the best of your ability, it leaves you with a great sense of achievement.

G.N.P. Golf Design Pty Ltd
Robina, Queensland, Australia

Par-5
MEN'S: 523 Metres
WOMEN'S: 449 Metres
DESIGNER: Graham Marsh (1985)

PALM MEADOWS
523m - par 5 - 18th hole

daring 'Davis' line

'Strange' safety line

GNP.
13/12/03

Essex Golf & Country Club, Canada

Sixteenth hole Jeff Mingay

As we all know, golf holes are played from tee to green. But in most cases, design strategy is more easily interpreted in reverse. In other words, the most advantageous fairway positions from where to approach specific hole locations are usually more clearly identifiable when standing behind the green. This adage especially applies for cleverly designed two-shot holes, looking back toward the tee.

Take the example of the 388-yard par-four, sixteenth hole at Essex Golf & Country Club in Canada, where in 1928–9 legendary golf architect Donald Ross designed a brilliant green complex that transformed a flat and rather uninspiring suburban farmland into a strategic golf hole.

Built up several feet above the level of the fairway with material excavated from a series of drainage swales throughout the property, Essex's sixteenth green was originally some 7,000 square feet in size, and featured elongated corners typical of Ross's design style of the late-1920s. Most notable, though, was a distinct lobe of green surface that jutted between two bunkers on the right-hand side. When holes were cut on that shallow portion of putting surface, golfers were well advised to drive down the extreme left-hand side of the fairway in order to open up a comparatively unimpeded angle to the flagstick.

Conversely, when the flagstick was located atop a high terrace in the green's back-left section—flanked by two bunkers with a steep fall-out at rear—a tee-shot down the right-hand side of the sixteenth fairway was mandatory to more easily gain access to the flagstick with one's approach. Playing angles were particularly important in the era prior to comprehensive watering, when the turf at Essex, and elsewhere, was more frequently impoverished. One direct consequence of the ground's firmness was that golfers had to pitch the ball short of the green into order to remain on its surface.

This type of strategy, dictated by the slope, contour, angle, and orientation of the putting green and its surrounding hazards, is also typical of Ross's work in the late-1920s throughout North America. Ross consistently tried to inject a mental element into the sport: to lift it above one that is merely an inherently physical test by at least prodding players into executing each stroke with the next in mind. At holes such as Essex's sixteenth, it was the golfer's responsibility to identify the position of the flagstick on any given day, then to drive accordingly.

In accordance with Ross's paper plan for the hole, Essex's sixteenth was to feature a fairway in excess of forty yards across, defended by four bunkers set between 110 and 150 yards off the tee on the fairway's right-hand side. Understanding the game was more difficult with long clubs, Ross consistently provided golfers with a wide berth off the tee. He then increased the challenge as play progressed toward the hole. Curiously, such blatant width tends to lull careless golfers into thinking any tee-shot finishing on the short grass will do. Only upon arriving at the ball in the fairway do such carefree golfers come to realise that they've played themselves out of position, and thus face a comparatively difficult approach to the hole.

Ross didn't entirely let high-handicappers, short-hitters, and errant drivers off the hook. At Essex's sixteenth, he placed two bunkers some thirty or forty yards short of the green, in the direct line to the hole. These bunkers—the style of which frequently feature at other Ross-designed courses—have been mischaracterised as 'deception bunkers' intended to confuse a golfer's distance perception. But, in fact, they are intended to eliminate mindless lay-up shots by those unable to reach the green on the fly. Ross figured that such golfers should also have a strategic decision to make.

Sadly, however, a conspiracy of sorts has been allowed to run unchecked. Club members, course superintendents, golf architects, and natural evolution, have undermined Ross's original design. Tree-encroachment, and a significant loss of fairway width and green-surface area, has gradually transformed Essex's sixteenth into a comparatively one-dimensional hole that today places unbalanced emphasis on driving straight through a narrow corridor.

No longer can thoughtful players drive down the right-hand side of the fairway, striving to gain access to the green's back-left, high-terraced pin positions.

Par-4
MEN'S: 388 Yards
WOMEN'S: 375 Yards
DESIGNER: Donald J. Ross (1928-29)

Ross's original fairway bunkers were removed during the mid-1960s, and, some twenty years later, three new bunkers were installed between 230 and 250 yards off the tee along the fairway's right-hand side. As a result, the fairway has narrowed significantly, and shifted left. And, although the option of driving down the extreme left-hand side of the fairway remains intact, there's no longer a strategic reason to do so. The distinctive lobe of putting surface that jutted between the right-hand side bunkers has also disappeared. Moreover, tree limbs overhang on both sides of the fairway, constricting play through the green to an excessively narrow corridor. No longer can one find alternate routes of play based on the location of the flagstick. The only option off the tee is to drive straight between rows of trees onto a sliver of fairway, or else face pitching out sideways from the forest back into the open with your next stroke.

In its original concept, Essex's sixteenth hole provided a case study on how to create something interesting out of almost nothing by simply building a green complex that rewarded thoughtful, strategic play into the green, coupled with opportunity for challenging and clever recovery shots from its surrounds. And its plight over the past half-century illustrates how simple it is to restore greatness to a hole suffering from the negative effects of tinkering and time. The solution is no mystery: expand the playing area; cut a few trees; reclaim lost putting surfaces; recontour the fairway according to the strategy dictated by the green complex—even if it involves removing a few non-original bunkers added after the fact; and water more judiciously in an attempt to cultivate a lively playing surface that enhances the strategic golf architecture already present. *Voila!* Golf is interesting again, thanks to a restoration of the ideas that forged Donald Ross's well-earned reputation of being a genius.

Rod Whitman Golf Course Design
Windsor, Ontario, Canada

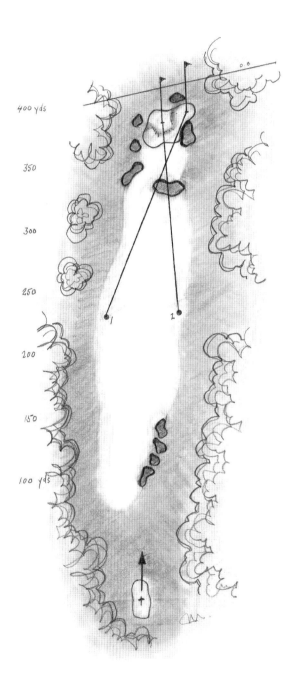

Royal Canberra Golf Club, Australia

Eighteenth hole Jamie Dawson

It may seem strange that a golf-course architect would nominate a straightaway par-five as a favourite hole. Perhaps stranger still: a straight hole with a huge green, and one where its only fairway bunker is rarely visited. I concede that such a nomination may fly in the face of current, good design convention—but what a hole!

From the drive, to the final putt, each of the shots is eminently fair, yet each can extract a lost shot, or two, if off-line. While standing on the eighteenth tee, a certain type of golfer could dismiss the looming shot as being not overly challenging. After all, there is no water, dense native grasses, doglegs, or massive bunkers, to avoid. The green is large and fully in view. But every hole has some danger, and with Royal Canberra's undulating eighteenth hole, it lurks in the form of the dense, tree-lined fairway margins, which penalise wayward shots.

The hole is lined by over twenty species of trees, with colourful, deciduous trees contrasting with the dominant Monterey pines and other conifers. Scanning this impressive scene, one's eye is led naturally to the clubhouse perched high above the eighteenth green. Royal Canberra is a fine, inland course, boasting over 200 diverse species of trees, which blend seamlessly and provide a wonderful setting to enjoy golf in the nation's capital. Against this backdrop, it's no surprise that Arnold Palmer once remarked that Royal Canberra is the course that most reminded him of Augusta National.

This hole is the one where I have personally witnessed the greatest amount of golfing triumph and tragedy. Being the climax of the round, it only exacerbates these possibilities. The comment is based upon thirty years of membership competing in Saturday competitions, plus enjoying the company of probably close to 1,000 golfers. And, of course, viewing tournaments has provided an additional perspective.

As the tee-shot landing zone is of medium width, most golfers feel at ease to open their shoulders and 'let one rip.' The batter-top—240 metres from the back tee—is well placed, as most club golfers will finish short of it. For the big-hitter, the batter downslope at 240 to 275 metres is strategically located, and may subject a player to a downhill lie. But there is also the enticement of a big kick forward, especially if it is reached on the full. Should this occur, the player's ball then runs into the valley around 285 metres from the tee. With good momentum, it might just climb the upslope to reach the 300-metre milestone. For powerful-hitting golfers, this provides an opportunity to reach this par-five in two shots—a 200-metre fairway-metal wood, or long-iron, to the green twelve metres above the fairway level—will do the trick.

After stringing together two fine shots, and being left with a short-iron third shot, golfers still need to execute their closing shots skilfully. For if the approach shot comes to rest on the far side of the over 800-square-metre green, then a three-putt scenario can unfold easily. A major tier of around 300 millimetres in height runs centrally across the green from the right. A shallower transition tier on the left, and a centreline tier at the back, further divides the large green into target zones, varying with the pin position. But get your approach shot close, and most putts are not overly difficult. However, when approaches settle a vast distance from the hole, tackling the various tiers and intervening slopes will force evaluation of a double-breaking putt, snaking every which way. I quite enjoy the challenge of these long putts with interesting lines, where the need for deft weight keeps one alert. Should a long putt finish tantalisingly close or, heaven forbid, go in, then an unashamed Tiger 'fist-pump' and big smile is a great way of finishing the round on a high.

The professionals and the crowds that enthusiastically line Royal Canberra's eighteenth hole have similarly experienced the highs and lows. Sadly, tournaments are all too infrequent at this great venue. At the 1980 Australia–Japan Foundation Trophy, and the 1988 ESP Open, much discussion centred upon just who could reach the eighteenth green with two big blows. The prime candidate at both events was the powerful and younger Greg Norman: on at least one occasion the 'Great White Shark' laced a staggering three-wood to the back of the green. Since the 1980s, the many technological advances to equipment has ensured that 'on in two' at Royal Canberra's eighteenth

> **Par-5**
> MEN'S: 511 Metres
> WOMEN'S: 411 Metres
> DESIGNER: John Harris (1962)

is now commonplace when tournaments are played. Notwithstanding, the cheer for such a feat remains just as vocal.

The impact of such technology at Royal Canberra is, perhaps, best exemplified by Brad King during the 1998 ANZ Tour Players Championship—on successive days he drove the ball over 300 metres from the eighteenth tee. To complete his third round, King's superb four-iron came to rest a mere fifteen centimetres from the cup for a tap-in eagle three. Playing the seventy-second hole with a one-stroke lead, and no doubt with adrenalin flowing, King launched a mammoth 313-metre drive, followed by an excellent five-iron onto the putting surface. Victory seemed assured. Unfortunately, he three-putted the green from below the major tier, as is a regular occurrence by the members. Mathew Goggin, meanwhile, hit a less impressive 275-metre drive, but then fashioned a great two-iron to the top tier. After making a birdie to force a play-off, the popular Tasmanian golfer again birdied the eighteenth hole—utilised as the first playoff hole—to win his first professional event.

The 1999 Championship is possibly best remembered by the changing fortunes of Australian professional Peter O'Malley, who led for most of the tournament. During the final round, his poor outward nine allowed other players back into contention. O'Malley arrived at the eighteenth tee with still some hope of victory, or at least a berth in a play-off. Alas, his drive found the woods on the left. I was standing only a few metres away from his attempted recovery shot, and what transpired—his ball ricocheting off a pine tree—was a sickening sight. It also led to a frenetic ball search. Eventually, O'Malley's ball was found in long grass behind more trees. Going from bad to worse, it took the ex-greenkeeper from Bathurst a few more shots to find the fairway. The whole experience was overwhelmingly disheartening for him, and his many supporters. Like a host of other locals, I've endured similar experiences to O'Malley on the eighteenth. My father long ago had a twelve to lose the club 'C' grade championship by a shot, yet, he's also holed many putts in excess of twenty

metres to wipe the assured smile of victory from opponents. O'Malley completed the hole in ten strokes, and finished well down the prize-money list. The winner of this drama-laden tournament was Marcus Cain.

As it has proved many times, the tee-shot on this exciting hole is pivotal to one's fortunes. But the eighteenth hole doesn't hang its hat solely on this shot—common to all shots along the way, disaster is never far away should a golfer's execution be sloppy. Moreover, golfers can experience triumph and tragedy on what is essentially a fair hole.

Enviro Links Design Pty Ltd
Phillip, Australian Capital
Territory, Australia

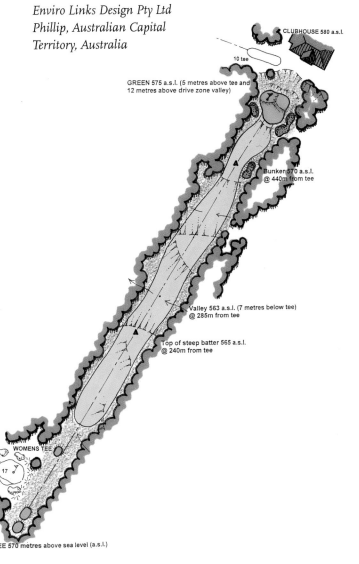

CLUBHOUSE 580 a.s.l.

10 tee

GREEN 575 a.s.l. (5 metres above tee and 12 metres above drive zone valley)

Bunker 570 a.s.l. @ 440m from tee

Valley 563 a.s.l. (7 metres below tee) @ 285m from tee

Top of steep batter 565 a.s.l. @ 240m from tee

WOMENS TEE

17

MENS TEE 570 metres above sea level (a.s.l.)

Cypress Point Club, USA
Seventeenth hole Robin Nelson

There are a number of reasons why this Cypress Point par-four is my favourite hole. First and foremost, the setting is one of the most spectacular on earth, and its gift to the senses is unequalled. Set along the cliffs of rocky peninsulas in the middle of the Pacific Coast, the scenery alone is enough to claim this hole as one of the most beautiful places one could ever hope to experience. The crashing, crystal white and foaming surf; the brisk ocean breeze; the barking of the sea lions; the smell of the salt air; the juxtaposition of the turf, trees, sand, and rock—all add to the spiritual experience a golfer receives when fortunate enough to play on this revered ground.

The hole comes at the end of one of golf's most spectacular and exciting three-hole stretches, namely, the fifteenth—a short, downhill par-three over a churning grotto, to an island among sprawling bunkers set in an amphitheatre of twisted, gnarled cypress trees. Then, of course, there's the colossal sixteenth hole—one of the most famous and photographed par-threes in the world with its 230-yard carry over the Pacific Ocean to a distant green. Clearly, this is a hard act to follow, and one would never expect anything to top that!

Once on the seventeenth tee, however, one finds even more excitement in store: a challenge that calls for two perfect shots to reach the precipice of a green, some 393 yards away. The green complex is angled so that attacking it from the fairway's far-left side creates a more open approach. The shorter, but significantly more risky option is to fire your tee-shot toward the fairway's right-hand side—as close to the cliffs of the ocean as possible. Choosing which route, and actually getting the ball to either of those points, is a cause for much soul-searching while on the tee.

The tee-shot can be negotiated in a variety of ways. Reaching the fairway requires a solid 'poke' over the crashing surf and rocky cliffs to an angled, sloping fairway. A magnificent group of old and weathered Cypress trees sits along the right edge of the fairway on the cliff, causing the golfer to attempt one of three types of tee-shots outlined. Depending on the golfer's skill, courage, and standing in his match, they can pinpoint an iron to a precise spot along the edge of the cliff on the right side of the fairway, short of the trees. This tee-shot strategy leaves the shortest route to the green, but creates a difficult and shallow approach as the green is also angled in harmony with the cliff. A relatively 'safe' tee-shot to the middle of the fairway, may leave the golfer behind the impervious Cypress trees, and virtually 'block-out' any direct avenue to the green. A third option is to attempt to crush a long drive and get past the trees; successfully achieved, one is left with a reasonably short approach. Yet another payoff: the green is more receptive with this option. The danger here, of course, is that the left side of the fairway tapers down by a forest of Cypress trees. And, naturally, the longer the tee shot, the smaller the fairway becomes, as the trees reduce the available landing area. Regardless of which tee-shot strategy is adopted, the approach shot will feel not unlike playing one of the trickiest par-threes in the world. It is rare that the ocean breezes are not a significant factor, and the green is surrounded by sand and ice plant. Only after two well-conceived and perfectly executed shots, aided by a bit of old-fashioned luck, will any chance for a birdie or par present.

Upon completion of the marvellous seventeenth hole at Cypress Point, one can reflect that a golfing treat has been devised by the best of what nature, and Dr Alister Mackenzie, could offer. I have never yet met the golfer who after putting out hasn't felt the strongest urge to march straight back to the tee and play it again. This is an entirely understandable reaction, for it may just be the finest par-four in the world.

Nelson & Haworth, Golf Course Architects
Mill Valley, California, USA

Par-4
MEN'S: 393 Yards
WOMEN'S: 355 Yards
DESIGNER: Alister Mackenzie (1927)

Cypress Point Club: Seventeenth hole, USA.
(Photo by Larry Lambrecht, LC Lambrecht Photography.)

County Louth Golf Club, Ireland

Fourteenth hole Tom Mackenzie

This nomination—a short, par-four on a great and underrated links—says as much about my feeling on golf, as the detail of the architecture. It is bunkerless, and was designed by the architect with, perhaps, the clearest vision of strategic golf design and its intrinsic merits. My hole of choice is the fourteenth at County Louth, or Baltray, as most prefer to call it.

The raw quality of the hole was the reason for this selection, but a peripheral reason is the approach to the course. Coming off the Dublin to Belfast road, you battle through the bustling streets of Drogheda, through the docks, past the concrete factory, and suddenly you are free, winding down the banks of the River Boyne past bays and mudflats. The dunes appear gradually on the final approach as you enter the hamlet of Baltray. It is a complete escape.

Like many links, Baltray surrenders few views of the sea, however, the fourteenth tee sits high above the long beach, looking out over the Irish Sea. It would be wrong, however, to start any description from the tee; in common with every great hole, the green is the making of the strategy. Here, the genius of architect Tom Simpson is there for all golfers to witness.

The green, which is undoubtedly a landmark in links design, is positioned upon a small, relatively steep-sloping plateau, which is long and narrow. To its right, the edge of the green pitches and tosses through a series of humps and rolls, diving off into sculptured hollows. To its left, there is a steep slope that drops at least four metres below the putting surface. Guarding the green at the front, lies a steep, grassy knob—more effective than any bunker—that is profoundly influential on approach play. Cunningly positioned, it is set back sufficiently from the front of the green to bluff you into dropping the ball too short. When this occurs, balls predictably bound off to one side, or another. The hummock is just high enough to catch more than its share of shots; in trying to avoid this situation, golfers can all too easily over-hit their approach shot and end up with a near-impossible pitch back down the green.

Simpson wrote eloquently and unambiguously about golf-course architecture, especially on the matter of technology and its adverse effects on the game. He believed passionately that strategic courses with creatively shaped greens could hold technology at bay, and the fourteenth hole at Baltray proves the point beyond all reasonable doubt.

More than ever, golfers must deliberate over their tee-shot. Titanium drivers, and new generation balls, have brought the green within range for the gifted, and many others can get close. Maybe so, but the reward is only there for those who can stay straight. The cardinal sin is missing the fairway to the right. This leaves a 'nervy' pitch—probably from a hanging lie—across the angle of the green and its contours. It is not an impossible pitch, but considerable touch is required: exactly what great, short par-fours are all about.

The green itself is a treacherous affair that walks a tightrope between fair, and unfair. The balance has been altered since Simpson's day, due to the faster green speeds of the past few decades, yet it still makes sense. It tumbles down from back-to-front, in a series of shallow shelves, connected by slippery slopes. If you do not stop your approach shot within ten or fifteen feet, a single putt is unlikely to result. The fourteenth at Baltray is a hole where even the best golfers will make as many bogeys as birdies, especially if the green is firm, as is invariably the case. What more can you ask of a bunkerless, short par-four?

Remember the name Tom Simpson: he may not have received the kudos of Donald Ross, Alister Mackenzie, or Harry Colt, but any student of design must study his writings and see his work. That leaves Baltray: it may lack the superlatives heaped on the likes of Ballybunion and Royal County Down but it is, without doubt, in the highest bracket of all links.

Donald Steel & Company Ltd
International Golf Course Architects
Chichester, West Sussex, England

Par-4
MEN'S: 332 Yards
WOMEN'S: 247 Yards
DESIGNER: Tom Simpson (1892)

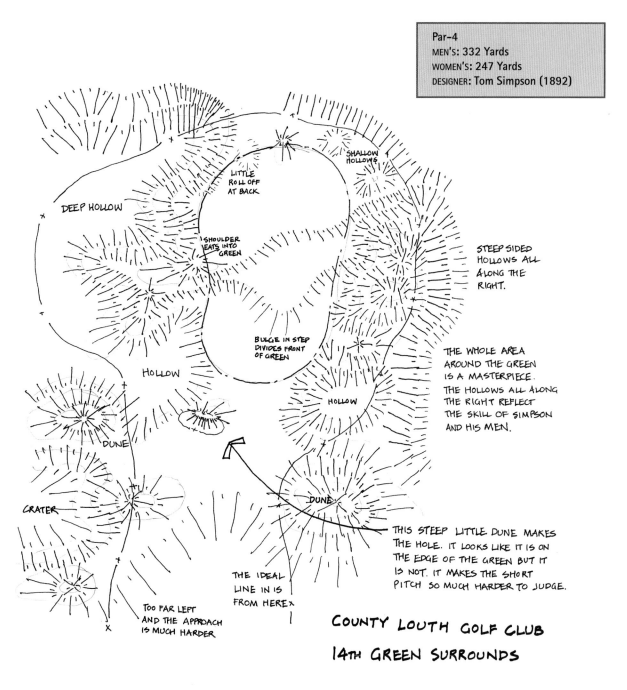

DEEP HOLLOW

LITTLE ROLL OFF AT BACK

SHALLOW HOLLOWS

SHOULDER EATS INTO GREEN

STEEP SIDED HOLLOWS ALL ALONG THE RIGHT.

BULGE IN STEP DIVIDES FRONT OF GREEN

HOLLOW

HOLLOW

THE WHOLE AREA AROUND THE GREEN IS A MASTERPIECE. THE HOLLOWS ALL ALONG THE RIGHT REFLECT THE SKILL OF SIMPSON AND HIS MEN.

DUNE

CRATER

DUNE

THIS STEEP LITTLE DUNE MAKES THE HOLE. IT LOOKS LIKE IT IS ON THE EDGE OF THE GREEN BUT IT IS NOT. IT MAKES THE SHORT PITCH SO MUCH HARDER TO JUDGE.

THE IDEAL LINE IN IS FROM HERE×

TOO FAR LEFT AND THE APPROACH IS MUCH HARDER

**COUNTY LOUTH GOLF CLUB
14TH GREEN SURROUNDS**

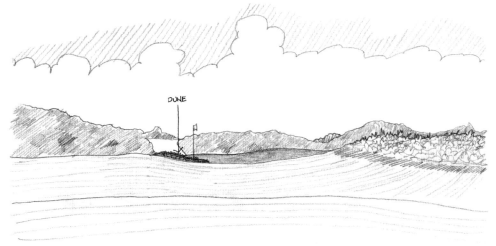

DUNE

County Louth Golf Club: Fourteenth hole, Ireland.
(Photo by Larry Lambrecht, LC Lambrecht Photography.)

Bethpage State Park, USA
Fourth hole: Black Course Richard Mandell

There was a trilogy of qualities that the great landscape architect, Frederick Law Olmsted, achieved in all his works. The notion of 'picturesque' came from his preservation of the wilder and rougher qualities of a site. The 'sublime' was achieved by preserving a great and awesome setting, while 'beautiful' was best defined by Olmsted as pastoral, spacious stretches of turf, quiet streams, and open groves of trees. Olmsted's great work of the nineteenth century was Central Park, and it has a twentieth century equivalent with golf architect A. W. Tillinghast's work at Bethpage State Park on Long Island, New York. Like Central Park, Bethpage was a stunning victory for the New York Parks Commission, which preserved acres of open space and provided countless New Yorkers with recreational opportunity. It is at Bethpage's five golf courses, and specifically throughout the Black Course, where I'm struck by the landscape qualities captured by Tillinghast—the very same ones that Mr Olmsted worked so hard to reveal in his works.

Nowhere is a site's natural character better displayed in a golf course routing than at Bethpage Black. All eighteen holes meld beautifully, and the routing is outstanding. In my opinion, the fourth exceeds them all. This is an excellent example of one hole brimming with picturesque, sublime, and beautiful features: all doled-out in equal portions. Picturesque is where the rough areas recede into the rugged treeline, peppered with golden hues on top of rock-outcroppings. Sublime is simply the tremendous view from a narrow wood downhill and beyond into an open meadow setting. The contrast of twisting, green fairway and white sand, illustrates the beautiful.

Surprisingly though, 'awe' and 'challenge' are the terms that best explain my fondness for the fourth hole. In describing the experience, one must begin on the third hole, which is surrounded by trees, giving little advance knowledge of the true character of this fantastic piece of property. Upon putting out on the third green, and turning toward the fourth tee, one of the most fantastic views in golf is revealed to the golfer. It is this view that encapsulates picturesque, beautiful, and sublime. Tillinghast's textbook example of a strong par-five—fully utilising the best natural qualities of the rolling Long Island topography—awaits all golfers. Personally, nothing could ever match the sense of wonderment when I first experienced this turn, yet it is still as breathtaking today. The thrill is achieved without an ocean or mountains: just high point, to ridge, to ridge, to high point.

As stunning as the fourth hole appears visually, it is primarily its existence as an architectural marvel—one that has stood the test of time and technology—that impresses me more. The reason it has so successfully remained relevant over the years, in spite of equipment advances by the manufacturers, is found in the cross-bunkering, partially 'blind' fairway areas, and a putting green that is tilted away from all approach shots. These elements make it mandatory for golfers to employ thoughtful shotmaking, over brute strength. I have worn out Max Behr's mantra: 'The direct line is the line of instinct, and if we wish to make a hole interesting, we must break up that line and create the line of charm,' always picturing Bethpage Black's fourth hole.

The teeing-ground is located in a narrow chute of woods and steps down the hillside. From the tee, a grand fairway bunker is set into the left hillside, creating a turn in that direction of this Tillinghast 'elbow' hole. Beyond the first landing area lies a second bunker, even grander than the first. Along with a smaller bunker to its far right, the bunker extends almost from treeline to treeline, and delineates the ground from the lower, first landing area, to a higher, second landing area. This bunker is the epitome of Tillinghast and his larger-than-life persona, plus his undoubted design talent. It fits naturally into the land and serves as a focal point for the golf hole, where no undue earthwork was required to make it work. The hazard helps to define landing areas, and assists in simple grade change. Its enormity is in proper scale with the bucolic scenery of the golf hole and creates a great *patte d'oie* technique: 'fool the eye.' It is so large and impressive that many first-timers to the Black are deceived into thinking it is reachable from the tee. In fact, it is about 370 yards away! The detailed, haphazard placement of the capes and bays further add to the expressive nature of this bunker.

From the tee, the golfer can shorten the hole by shaping their tee-shot from right to left, drawing as close

Par-5
MEN'S: 522 Yards
WOMEN'S: 436 Yards
DESIGNER: A. W. Tillinghast (1934–35)

to the first fairway bunker as possible. However, a drive of 245 yards can end up in the sand. Yet be aware: this 'line of instinct' isn't as charming if one strays too far to the left. For a ball positioned down that side does shorten the second shot, but it leaves the golfer completely 'blind.' One extra deterrent: it's more of an acute angle should you wish to reach the green in two. On many occasions after reaching the fairway and deciding to cut the left side short, I've pulled my second shot sufficiently left to find myself blocked by the trees, or finished fifty feet below the green with no view of the flagstick. Tillinghast utilised the natural topography to create challenge and defence along this 'line of instinct.' The further right that one places one's tee-shot, the more the second landing area and green opens up to full view. The angle of approach for the second and third shots is considerably more favourable from the right-hand side of the fairway.

The second landing area begins at the top of the second fairway bunker, and covers the last 140 yards to the green. A front-left, greenside bunker creates a twist in the fairway, and Tillinghast so often specified this in his design work. The fairway meets the green along the longer route down the right side. Although the green is

stationed level with the rising plateau fairway, it is well protected on three sides by severe slopes. A further complication is that the fourth green pitches away from the golfer. This keeps golfers painfully aware of the consequences of rolling off the back of the green, down the hill, and into the woods. The design of the green makes it receptive to smart short-iron play, far more so than most will be able to produce with a long-iron, or fairway metal-wood.

The fourth hole at Bethpage State Park's Black Course is a great example where natural topography can create strategy, as well as acting as a defence against unbridled technological advances. Tillinghast's forethought back in 1936 has withstood the threats of time and progress. His ability to develop this hole while preserving the beautiful, picturesque, and sublime qualities of the land is what makes this hole my favourite to walk with clubs in hand. Thanks, Tilly.

*Richard Mandell Golf Architecture
Pinehurst, North Carolina, USA*

Mudgee Golf Club, Australia

Seventeenth hole James Wilcher

When asked to nominate my favourite golf hole, several candidates immediately spring to mind: the sixteenth hole at Cypress Point; the ninth at Pebble Beach; the sixth at New South Wales; and the ninth at Royal County Down. But, in truth, having played so few courses—relative to the number available—it is a difficult proposition to support just one golf hole. For the sake of the exercise, though, the following nine points represent my personal criteria for a favourite hole:

1. The hole must have a historic element to it.
2. It should be playable in virtually any conditions.
3. It should fall preferably within a stretch of strong holes.
4. It should not necessarily require the use of the driver.
5. It should, regardless of conditions, make club choice difficult.
6. It should be strikingly attractive.
7. The pin position should have a bearing on how the hole is played.
8. It should be a hole that yields as many birdies as double-bogeys.
9. Above all, it should encourage some reward for taking risks.

For the well-travelled golfer, Mudgee's seventeenth hole might seem like an unlikely choice, when the world beckons. It has been said a thousand times: beauty is in the eye of the beholder, and this golf hole is an absolute treat. If one was experiencing its charms and machinations in the middle of a round at Cypress Point, or, dare I say, Pine Valley, it would hardly seem out of place. Indeed, it would be the equal of any hole found on either course.

Applying the criteria stated above, the par-three, seventeenth hole at Mudgee would make everybody's shortlist. During my process of elimination, it seemed entirely appropriate to select a hole that is not heralded as 'one of the greats' but, rather, one that should be recognised under this banner.

Mudgee is a lovely country town found in the central west of New South Wales—a region noted more for its exceptional wines than for its golf courses. As with many of the smaller country towns around Australia, golf is a pastime enjoyed on courses of varying quality. Once in a while, however, you strike a course of exceptional pedigree, and this is the case with Mudgee Golf Club. Fortunately, the site is ideal for golf, rolling alongside a meandering creek that comes 'into play' on nine holes: a most interesting property. I'm unsure as to whether Dan Soutar—Mudgee's course architect—had the luxury of choosing his site—an atypical situation—but, if so, his influence could not have been more beneficial to the golfing landscape in Mudgee.

From the first, to the last hole, this layout intrigues with its eclectic presentation of holes, arranged in such a manner as to give every club in your bag a workout. On very few holes is one forced to select a driver from the tee, or find it too obviously suggested as the club of choice. Thankfully for the Mudgee locals, they are spared the negative effects of this tedious golfing paradigm. In my opinion, a golf course that relies on the paradigm cannot ever hope to stand the test of time. Too often, many great golf holes have required constant change to defend itself from the longer hitter. Other than a couple of the par-fives, I'm struggling to think of any Mudgee holes that have been spoilt, lessened, or ruined by the advances in club and ball technology.

To be classified as a great hole, ideally one's nomination should lie within a group of great holes. I categorise the following as stunning examples of three-hole stretches: the eleventh through thirteenth holes at Augusta; the fourteenth to sixteenth at New South Wales; Cypress Point's fifteenth to seventeenth; and the seventh through ninth holes at Lahinch. In the case of Mudgee's seventeenth hole, it lies within a similarly impressive stretch: the sixteenth through eighteenth holes. And as these are the finishing holes, they can either make, or mar, your round. My guess is that for Mudgee members, both scenarios have been played out equally over the years. Individually, each of the holes can be considered a birdie opportunity. Conversely, each regularly throws up double-bogies, with just a solitary mistake. On balance: defensive play should not be a consideration when closing out your round at Mudgee.

'Donga'
Par–3
MEN'S: 127 Metres
WOMEN'S: 120 Metres
DESIGNER: Dan Soutar (1911)

The seventeenth hole plays from an elevated tee, offering an unobliterated view of the danger that awaits the golfer. An attractive creek after which the hole has been named—the Donga—must be carried if the green is to be found. The creek, itself, runs at a forty-five degree angle to the line of play, until it almost sidles up to the front, left-hand side of the green. So attacking a pin positioned on the left is a vastly different proposition to attacking a right-side pin. Additionally, immediately behind the left-hand side of the green is a high mound. The creek and mound combined, ensure that golfers are confronted with an area no more receptive than Royal Troon's famous 'Postage Stamp' green. So when the pin is placed in the front, left-hand portion of the green, a tee-shot only several metres short of the putting surface will find the dreaded 'Donga.' And, any shot that is a few metres too long, will see the ball finish on the wrong side of the mound. From this position, a golfer's predicament is precarious to say the least: getting your ball up-and-down is really a case of more good luck than good management. As the hole is without a bunker, to some it may appear to be a pushover should the 'Donga' be avoided. However, the right-hand side of the hole is decidedly unfriendly territory, being a wasteland of grass and trees. Finding a reasonable and playable lie in this area is as rare as a triple-bogey from Tiger Woods. The fairway is so small it makes a cricket pitch look big, so when all is said and done, missing the seventeenth green is almost never kind to your score.

Golf architects, such as Dan Soutar deserve our praise and acknowledgment, for the art of golf-course design should always be about capturing the best the site has to offer. At Mudgee, Soutar has done this to perfection, as anyone who has played the seventeenth hole will testify readily.

Golf by Design
Gordon, New South Wales, Australia

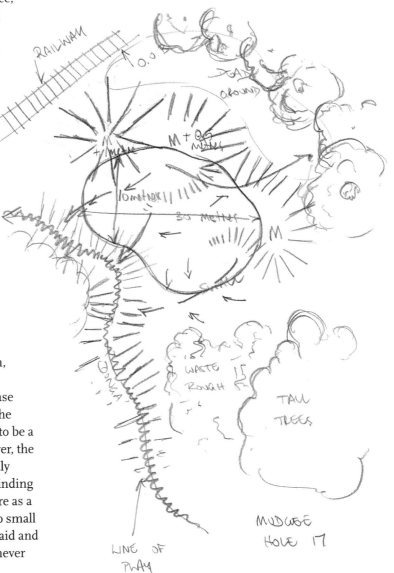

The Valley Club, USA

Fifteenth hole Forrest Richardson

During high school I tried out for the golf team. With all my other activities, life became a difficult juggling act. Attending practice sessions every Tuesday, Wednesday, and Thursday, ensured that at least nine holes and a few-hundred range balls were under my belt each week. Occasionally, schoolwork suffered, but I was okay with that. Golf prevailed.

We played at two courses: The Arizona Biltmore Adobe Course, a 1928 layout of William P. 'Billy' Bell; and The Valley Club, a 1957 design by David Gill. Our team was broken into two divisions, and those with the best stroke averages played at the Abode Course—I only hovered in this group a few times. Mostly, I played at The Valley Club.

The Valley Club was a classic design; it followed the land, was built with minimal earthwork and very little in the way of landscaping. Gill built the course for a resort that was set on the slopes of Camelback Mountain—a red rock and cactus covered landmark in the heart of Phoenix. The front nine was predominantly flat. The back nine, however, was of an entirely different character. The holes situated between the eleventh and eighteenth ascended up some seventy to eighty feet, and then dropped that much toward the final green. The fifteenth hole was smack in the middle of this roller-coaster ride.

Gill's creation of The Valley Club's fifteenth hole consisted of a large teeing ground, which was directly at the toe of the eastern slope of Camelback Mountain. Here, some 1,500 feet below Camelback's craggy peak, was a tee facing a steep slope. Golfers unfamiliar with the routing would often inquire which direction the hole set off. Upon being told, they often uttered the same exclamation: 'Wow!'

Play was essentially uphill—very much so. The green, a modest-sized oval shape, had been lovingly carved from the steep slope, as if it was planned that a home might eventually be built there. Much of the slope facing the tee had been planted with grass, and there was a gentle desert arroyo crossing in front of the tees. Saguaro cactus and desert trees dotted the sides, while behind the elevated green, one could easily be awed by the sight of large red rocks and the undisturbed mountain slope.

Although the hole—indeed the entire original course created by Gill—is no longer in existence, I can recall the fifteenth hole with crystal clear clarity—as if I had played it just last week. The green's surface was completely out of view from the tee. An extra long flagstick—I swear nearly nine feet tall—was always visible, albeit, sometimes only the tip when the hole location was at the rear. The green was mostly of gentle undulation, with a small punchbowl feature at the left. Behind the green there was a swale to catch the torrential rains, which could pour down the hill. On both sides of the green there were steep drop-offs. Balls left, or right, of the green would bound away from play as if someone had been engaged to stand guard and toss such shots to the desert brush a few seconds after they had been struck.

Why did this hole stand out? I suppose it is because it is among a handful of holes, which, even today, have always perplexed me. Gill's layout directed the golfer go directly up a mountainside with a short par-three: a rare occurrence! The question of what made him do this still haunts me. It was always such fun to strike a tee-shot and then anxiously await the outcome. At most par-threes, we hit and know almost instantly the fate of our shot. Did Gill anticipate this extra game of 'wait and see?' That question also haunts me.

I might point out that there were no formal hazards at the fifteenth hole—formal hazards were simply not necessary. Gill was a smart designer. He knew when enough was enough. Here, he had bestowed a fascinating tee shot—one that is surely a rare experience—and he relied on the mountain

Hole and course now defunct
Par–3
MEN'S: 135 Yards
WOMEN'S: 115 Yards
DESIGNER: David Gill (1957)

to offer the ground game to those wanting to play in that manner. Tee-shots too far to the right, or left, could be rendered unplayable. The risky shot to a forward pin might not be a sensible option, for sometimes a ball not reaching the top of the crest at the front of the green would dribble aimlessly back toward the tee. I can still remember laughing at my fellow team-mates when this occurred. And it is my guess, although such memories are naturally blocked, that they, too, laughed at me.

David Gill was a friend. Before his passing, I recall great conversation about golf and golf architecture. In particular, I regret not having a specific conversation about this hole. Perhaps the quirky nature of it was a fearful subject, and just how would I ever broach the topic: 'Say, David, what in God's name made you route that hole thirty feet up a steep hillside?' I never asked and he never said.

Forrest Richardson & Associates
Golf Course Architects
Phoenix, Arizona, USA

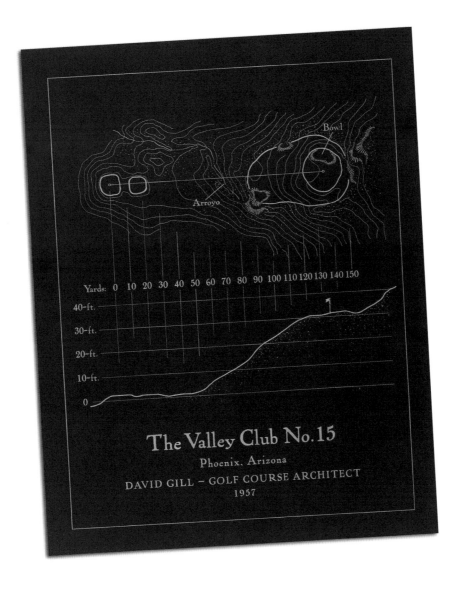

Yards: 0 10 20 30 40 50 60 70 80 90 100 110 120 130 140 150

The Valley Club No. 15
Phoenix, Arizona
DAVID GILL – GOLF COURSE ARCHITECT
1957

Royal Dornoch Golf Club, Scotland
Eighth hole Shunsuke Kato

Until replaced by earthmoving equipment around the turn of the twentieth century, golf courses were built mostly by human endeavour. Obviously, the types of courses produced were dictated by natural terrain. Success hinged mainly upon three issues: selecting a site optimally suited for a fine course; the ability to build it; and having a superior routing that led to an enjoyable golfing experience.

Located in the far north of Scotland, Dornoch was no doubt seen as an ideal site for golf, and in spite of its remote locality, it attracts visitors from far and wide.

As a golf-course architect, I regard the eighth hole at Royal Dornoch as its signature hole and also my favourite hole in golf.

To be considered outstanding, ideally any golf hole should meet a number of conditions. First, there is the 'wind' factor, and how its presence impacts upon the playability of that hole, and players' enjoyment. As the saying goes: 'No wind, no golf!' On many of the world's greatest courses, you find that the presence of wind increases the pleasure of playing golf. Second, any hole worth its grain of salt should invoke a thinking response from the player. Third, it should provide the player with the pleasure of 'reading' the course. Additionally, in order for it to rate in the top league, it must also score heavily in several areas: shot value; strategic design; visual appeal; and memorability.

Royal Dornoch's par-four, eighth hole passes the test with flying colours, and has enough distance, even by today's standards, to remain relevant and challenging. It is more or less flat for the first 270 yards at the centre until it plunges steeply down to the lower level about fifty-to-sixty feet below. Guiding poles are located 300 yards on the left and 235 yards on the right, respectively. Once the lower section has been reached, the fairway slopes diagonally away to the right. This marked diagonal slant is the key to this hole.

For the all-important tee-shot, golfers must decide whether it's prudent to lay-up and remain on the upper level—leaving a downhill second shot carry over the rough—or attempt a daring, long tee-shot that trundles all the way down to the lower level. This second option, for those fortunate enough to indulge it, will leave the player with a short, lofted approach. For the shorter-hitting golfer, there is no real alternative: just hit a fine and straight tee-shot and stay on the upper level. Sound judgment, taking in the strength and fickleness of the wind, plus accounting for your hitting capability, is vital for achieving a good score on this hole.

Should you get away a lengthy tee-shot, the approach shot is lofted to a green—resting more than forty feet above your level—that falls away around the edges, and is flanked by two gaping sand bunkers. Interestingly, a side-elevation plan view of the hole reveals that the green and tee are more or less at the same level. It also depicts how, seemingly, a massive 'bite' has been taken out of the hole.

The eighth hole at Royal Dornoch features slopes running vertically and horizontally, so it's no wonder that golfers never tire of locking horns with it, and almost always find it challenging.

The sky and light of the northland with its exquisite changes are no less splendid than the golf course itself.

Kato World Inc.
Funabashi-shi, Chiba, Japan

'Dunrobin'
Par–4
MEN'S: 437 Yards
WOMEN'S: 380 Yards
DESIGNER: George Duncan (1947)

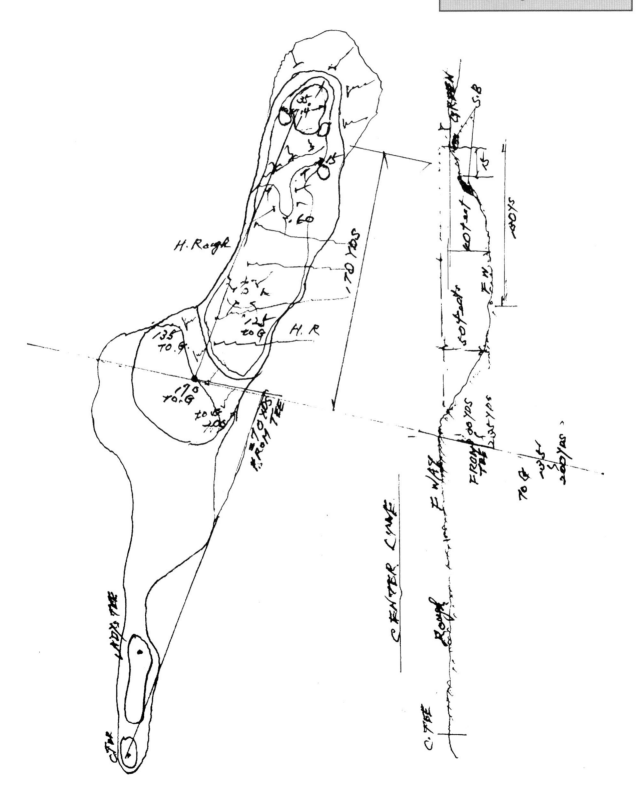

Merion Golf Club, USA

Sixteenth hole: East Course Dana Fry

The East Course at Merion in Ardmore, Pennsylvania, is, in my opinion, as well as many others, an architectural masterpiece. Designed by Hugh Wilson and opened for play in 1912, it is blessed with eighteen great holes that feature brilliantly placed bunkering throughout its layout. My personal favourite hole at Merion, and probably my favourite hole anywhere, is the sixteenth, known simply as the Quarry Hole.

The hole is a medium-length par-four, ranging in yardage from 428 to 356 yards depending on which set of tees you play from. The sixteenth tee is situated upon one of the highest points on the course, calling for a thrilling drive to the fairway below. Your view of where the ball will land is obscured, because the ground leading off from the tee remains relatively level for the first 100 yards before dropping about thirty-five to forty feet. The terrain then rises gently up to the old, abandoned rock quarry that comes into play over the final three holes. A small section of the fairway can be seen short of the quarry, which is misleading, because your instinct implores you to hit it there. Do so, and this folly will result in your ball being too far to the left and finishing in the rough. Having played Merion East several times, I have learned that it is far better to aim your drive out to the right, to enable a better approach angle into the green.

If the drive is positioned correctly, the second shot over the quarry can be as little as a short- or a medium-iron, to a green that sits slightly above the landing area. The quarry has a high face filled with bunkers, and extensive natural vegetation that is extremely difficult to play out of. Since 1912, the quarry has undergone several 'makeovers' during the course of its evolution. In recent times, trees and some vegetation have been removed to more closely capture its original look. As a by-product of the tree-removal, two additional approach options have become available, namely, a 'safe' aerial attack, and the ball being brought in from the right of the quarry. For those golfers previously not powerful enough to carry their seconds onto the putting surface, this change has been most welcome.

The green is large in size, but due to its contours, it effectively plays much smaller as pin positions are limited. Merion's sixteenth green makes an interesting study: a large bowl in the front-right of the green; the left-hand side of the green is narrow and elevated from the front; the back of the green is a couple of feet higher than the front, and reasonably level. Over the green, mounds and the troublesome Merion rough ensure that short-game recoveries are testing and never automatic. All this goes to reinforce that even though the approach shot is short, it is very demanding—especially when there is a lot riding on the outcome.

Merion has played host to many important championships through the years, and unusual things do have a way of occurring at this hole. One of these occurred during the 1950 US Open, which saw the return and triumph of one of golf's all-time greats, Ben Hogan. After seventy-two holes, Hogan was tied with George Fazio and Lloyd Mangrum, necessitating an eighteen-hole play-off. It was during this tense affair that the East's sixteenth hole played a decisive role in the outcome. After fifteen holes Hogan was one stroke ahead of Mangrum, and four ahead of Fazio. Hogan and Fazio hit good drives down the sixteenth fairway, but Mangrum's tee shot found the tall grass. After studying his lie and stance, the golfer known as the 'Riverboat Gambler' believed that he couldn't reach the green without going in the quarry. So he chipped out of the long grass onto the fairway, then hit his third shot to around fifteen feet from the cup. Ever the machine, Hogan rifled his second shot to barely six feet away. Mangrum marked his ball because it interfered with Fazio's putt, and then replaced it. Then just before settling into the serious business of putting, Mangrum noticed an insect on his ball. Once again, he picked up his ball, blew the insect away, replaced the ball, and bravely holed out for his four. Hogan missed his short birdie putt, while Fazio recorded a bogey five. To all and sundry, it appeared that Hogan held a one-stroke lead.

But before Mangrum had time to hit his tee-shot on the seventeenth hole, USGA Rules Chairman Issac Grainger informed him that a two-stroke penalty was to be applied for lifting his ball 'in play.' In the heat of the moment, Mangrum forgot to mark his ball before picking it up to blow away the insect. He had a six instead of a four. Now he trailed by three, not one. Clearly shaken, Mangrum finished with a seventy-three, to Fazio's seventy-five, against Hogan's winning score of sixty-nine. If you know this bit of history when playing the hole, you can almost feel the emotion that must have been generated here. For some it must be like visiting a hallowed battlefield.

In leaving this wonderful hole, perhaps it is apt to conclude with a quote from golf-course architect, A. W. Tillinghast, who summed it up most succinctly: 'No one will ever play Merion without taking away the memory of number sixteen.' I couldn't agree more, and I can't wait to play the sixteenth hole again, and again.

Hurdzan: Fry
Columbus, Ohio, USA

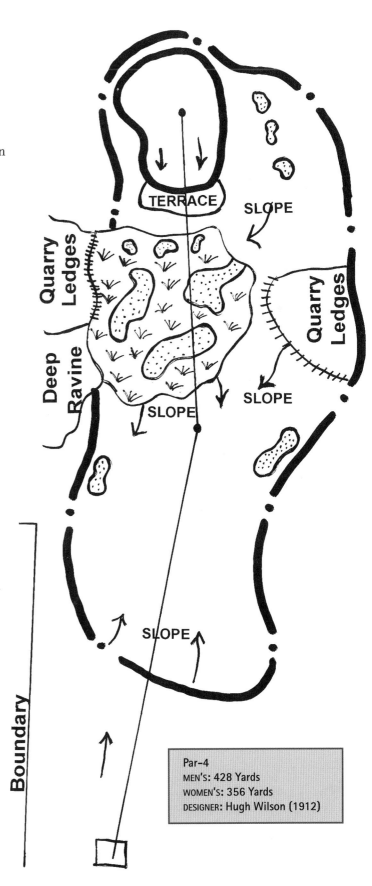

TERRACE

SLOPE

Quarry Ledges

Deep Ravine

Quarry Ledges

SLOPE

SLOPE

SLOPE

SLOPE

Boundary

Par-4
MEN'S: 428 Yards
WOMEN'S: 356 Yards
DESIGNER: Hugh Wilson (1912)

Royal Dornoch Golf Club, Scotland

Fourteenth hole Mark Thawley

Golfers have debated for centuries over what makes one golf hole better than another. Some have even come up with ways to determine rankings of the best holes in the world. This all makes for great conversation, and it sells magazines by the truckloads, but, for me, the greatest holes are quite simply the ones that are the most fun to play. Based on this simple standard, the fourteenth hole at Royal Dornoch must be considered among the finest in the world, and it is my favourite.

The fourteenth is named 'Foxy' probably because it is such a tricky hole to conquer, but the name may also be derived from its pure natural beauty. The view for the first-time visitor, however, can be deceiving. The low-profile landscape is devoid of any dramatic elevation changes, water features, or even sand bunkers. Instead, the fairway appears flat, and is defined only by a natural dune ridge that twists back and forth down its right-hand side. Eventually this ties into a four to six foot high plateau where the green is located.

Measuring 454 yards from the back tee, Foxy plays as a par-four and heads off in a southerly direction. Embo Bay is close by—just over a dune that runs along the left-hand side of the hole. The prevailing wind blows from the sea against the line of play and slightly left-to-right, making it a firm, two-shotter for the long-ball hitter, and most likely a three-shot hole for the shorter-hitter.

Many subscribe to the theory that the hole is a double-dogleg, even though the direct line of play is relatively straight. The winding nature of the dune ridge, with its pronounced promontories that jut out into the fairway, makes the hole feel as if it is turning more than it really is. This ridge, combined with the rough grass on the left that must be carried off the tee, helps to make 'Foxy' a great risk-and-reward hole.

A long drive into the slot located between the first promontory of the dune ridge on the right, and the rough grass on the left, will reward the golfer with extra roll, and a clear view of the green for the approach. Golfers who choose to play safely to the right, will need to tack back left into the wind for the second shot in order to avoid the next promontory located seventy yards from the green. From this position, the third shot must then play back to the right toward the green. Hence, the feeling of a double-dogleg. In a match-play situation, a shorter hitting competitor should never give up hope, as the plateau green acts as a great equaliser. A short-hitter who is skilled with a proficient 'ground' game, and possesses a deft touch on and around the green, has the opportunity to outsmart an overly aggressive long-ball hitter.

Relative to the line of play, the natural plateau where the green sits is much wider than it is deep. This aspect, combined with its tightly mown banks, promotes a challenging approach from any distance. The options are numerous. Some may attempt a high shot to the narrow-left section of the green, while others may think it prudent to 'bail' out to the right where there is more support. Another option is to lay-up to the left, so that the next shot can play into the long part of the green. Some imaginative and skilled golfers will navigate a low-running chip, or putt, using the steep bank to 'kill' the ball and 'coax' it up near the pin. This becomes even more precarious when the pin is cut to the middle, or right side, of the green, where an eight-foot bump in the bank will deflect all but the most perfectly struck approach.

Once on the green, a two-putt is no easy matter. Its subtle contours will challenge even the best putters. Even more interesting, are the edges of the green, which tie directly into the slope of the bank and make it possible for aggressive putts to run off the green and back down the slope. A humbling experience at best.

By the time golfers leave the fourteenth green, 'Foxy' is bound to have made an impression. It will have earned their respect as a cunning and challenging golf hole: one that can be played in many different ways. For today's architects, 'Foxy' remains a model of deceptive simplicity, where Dornoch's natural features have been utilised to create a hole that is always fun to play.

Kyle Phillips Golf Course Design
Granite Bay, California, USA

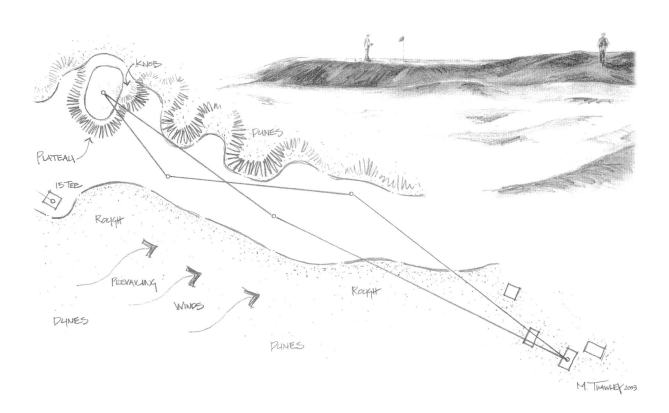

M. Thawley 2003

'Foxy'
Par-4
MEN'S: 454 Yards
WOMEN'S: 401 Yards (Par-5)
DESIGNER: Old Tom Morris (1877)

Royal Troon Golf Club, Scotland

Eighth hole Ron Garl

R oyal Troon Golf Club on the West Coast of Scotland has been venue for seven Open
Championships. It is a formidable links and the club's motto states precisely the
philosophy required during play: *'tam arte quam marte.'* Readers may be more familiar
with the translation: 'As much by skill as by strength.' Nowhere throughout the layout is
this motto more relevant than at its most celebrated hole, the short par-three 'Postage Stamp'
hole. As the shortest par-three in Open Championship competition—measuring only 126 yards
from the back tee—its design is deceptively simple. From an elevated teeing ground shaved
from the top of a large sand dune, the play is directed to a small, perched green carved into
another neighboring dune. The putting surface is just eight paces wide and surrounded by five
pot bunkers with a large sand dune to the left. The dune shelters the green, and makes the
wind's effect more difficult to read. Even among the storied collection of links holes in Britain
it is unique. There is no safe play; you're either on the green, or in trouble. The ball cannot be
trundled along the ground; it must be played high through the air. In many ways it may have
been the first 'island' green.

The setting of Royal Troon's eighth hole is almost without comparison, with views of the
Firth of Clyde and the Isles of Arran and Kintyre in the background. On a clear day, it is even
possible to see the northernmost tip of Ireland. But such days are few and far between. It is
said by the local Troonites that if you can't see the Isle of Arran from the Postage Stamp tee,
then it's raining, and if you can see it then it means it's about to rain. The elements play such
an influential role in links golf, and the Postage Stamp hole is no exception. Depending on the
wind direction and its strength, I have played anything from a three-iron to a wedge. What a
shame that more par-threes around the golfing globe cannot offer this variety of shotmaking.

The present eighth hole was designed in 1909—some thirty years after the club's conception.
The original eighth hole called for a blind tee-shot to a green behind the sand dune to the left of
the present green. From what one gathers, I've heard that the current design—the size of the
green in particular—received a lot of early criticism. The then golf correspondent at the
Glasgow Herald plastered his opinion around that the green was ridiculously small, and the
hole painfully difficult to play. Nonetheless, in the spring of 1910, the Great Triumvirate—Harry
Vardon, James Braid, and J. H. Taylor—played an exhibition match on the course that included
the new Postage Stamp hole. How comforting it must have been, shortly thereafter, for the club
to receive letters of support from the three greatest players in the game, expressing how they
thoroughly enjoyed and approved of the new addition.

No great hole will be without its critics, but I have always found this hole to be intriguing.
Its simplicity, setting, and potential calamity, sets it apart from all others in an age where so
many par-threes are no longer very short. It remains a unique and refreshing symbol of
defiance. Perhaps the twelfth at Augusta National aside, where else could a single hole produce
a score of fifteen—Herman Tissies in the 1950 Open—and a hole-in-one by seventy-one-year-
old Gene Sarazen in the 1973 Open Championship. Contemporary professionals are not spared
the trial, and even the great Tiger Woods took a triple-bogey six here on his first visit to Royal
Troon at the 1997 Open.

Love it or hate it, the Postage Stamp is a hole you just cannot forget. Ever since first playing
Troon in 1967, I have always enjoyed the challenge and pure fun of playing the Postage Stamp.

I designed the first replica golf course in the world, Golden Ocala. In recognition of the
impression that the Postage Stamp hole has made on me, it was incorporated into the layout

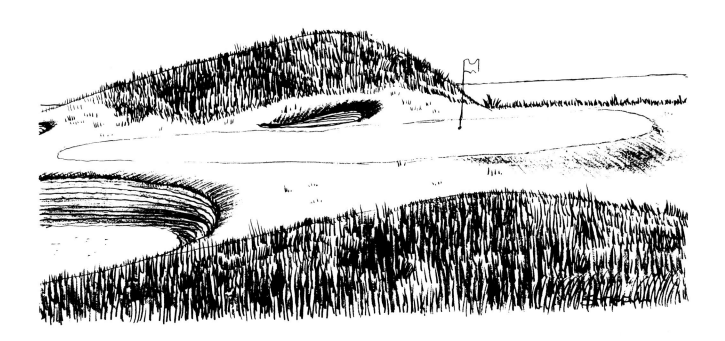

at Golden Ocala. The magazine, *Travel & Leisure* has ranked it as the Best Replica Course in the USA.

My senior design associate, Steven McFarlane, who is originally from Troon, joined our practice five years ago. This was the period when I was completing the construction of a replica of the Postage Stamp at Wooden Sticks Golf Club north of Toronto, Canada. I was especially keen for Steven to see the hole before it was grassed, to get his opinion upfront. When he stood on the tee, he remarked: 'The only thing missing was a forty-mile-an-hour wind and the backdrop of the Irish Sea.' I knew right then, that I had done all I could to pay homage to this great hole.

Ron Garl Golf Course Design
Lakeland, Florida, USA

'Postage Stamp'
Par-3
MEN'S: 126 Yards
WOMEN'S: 118 Yards
DESIGNER: Willie Fernie (1909)

Coto de Caza Golf & Racquet Club, USA

Seventeenth hole: North Course Casey O'Callaghan

There are two design elements that define the North Course at Coto de Caza Golf & Racquet Club, namely, being one of the toughest first-shot courses that I have played, and the greens possessing contours that are far from subtle. The equation is stark: you either learn to drive the ball accurately and read greens, or adjust to turning in high scores and paying for the drinks. Predominantly, the North Course is configured as 'out-and-back,' with the layout routed along an intermittent stream. Another feature is an existing forest of mature oak trees.

The North's par-four, seventeenth hole places a premium on accuracy from the tee, and the prevailing wind is up the canyon against the golf hole. Thankfully, the wind doesn't necessarily 'roar', being usually more of a steady breeze, and only occasionally a 'stiff' breeze. To present a snapshot of the hole: the riparian woodland plays as a lateral hazard and borders the entire left side of the golf hole. The stream running through this oak woodland is twenty feet below the fairway, and there are four small ravines within the golf turf limits that run from the right-hand side of the hole to the creek. The hole has a region to be hypervigilant about: Out of bounds on the right-hand side of the hole. There are no fairway bunkers on the seventeenth hole and none are needed. The green is situated above the fairway and it slopes from back to front. It has three distinct areas that are separated by two ridges, and the middle portion is slightly higher than the front-right and back-left portions. Four bunkers surround the green, however, it is the ones positioned at the front-middle, and the right-hand bunker, in which golfers most commonly find themselves bunkered. Finally, a beautiful and menacing solitary oak tree is located to the centre-right of the hole corridor, and it defines this hole.

Occasionally, one hears that holes with a solitary tree should not be classified as 'great.' Those who subscribe to this theory suggest it is because of the finite existence of that tree. The tree in question is approximately seventy years old, and it should live another hundred years—more than enough time for it to remain my favourite hole! The optimum fairway landing area runs from short, right—230 yards from the back tee—to longer on the left, where the fairway terminates at 300 yards from the back tee. The short, right-hand section of the fairway offers the greatest landing area width, and it is the safer shot off the tee. If the tee-shot veers too far to the right, the golfer's approach is compromised by the presence of the large oak tree. When this occurs, a 190-yard, 'cut' shot (for right-handed golfers) is required to make amends. This applies when the pin is on the front, right-hand side of the green, but increases to a 210-yard shot if the pin is back-left. The longer, left-hand section of the fairway offers the best approach to the green, but this option also presents the greatest risk from the tee. Obviously, not everyone can 'nail' the ball, but from the back tee the ideal drive is 270 yards, to a fairway that narrows down to around twenty-seven yards in width. Any tee-shot to the left—especially a right-hander's hook—may reach the woodland ravine.

The approach shot to the green from the far, left-hand side of the fairway is partially blocked by another smaller oak tree. The tree can usually be carried with a lofted club, or it may demand a shot played gently from right to left. I've noted that many long-hitting golfers end up 'bailing' out to the fairway's right-hand side—anything to avoid the lateral hazard. A tee-shot that is long and positioned on the right side of the fairway gives the golfer a close and unobstructed view of the defining oak tree. The tree is located in one of the small ravines within the turf limits, and any shot in this area funnels toward it. Then, one finds that the golfer's sidehill stance in deep rough, plus the looming tree, negates any realistic opportunity of reaching the green in two shots. One sound recovery option is to chip out sideways to the left, or if you are fortunate, orchestrate a short 'bunt' under the tree to the fairway, short of the green. The fairway cut terminates well short of the green, making way to a rough-covered upslope—five to eight feet above the fairway—rising to the green. This fact, allied to the presence of bunkers guarding the front of the green, makes it is virtually impossible to play a 'bump-and-run' shot toward the target. The hole is tough but playable: a perfect tee-shot is rewarded with an approach shot of between 140 and 160 yards to the green.

The seventeenth green is spacious, where as much as a three-club difference exists between the front,

Par-4
MEN'S: 427 yards
WOMEN'S: 333 yards
DESIGNER: Robert Trent Jones Jr. (1987)

right-hand portion of the green, and that of the back-left. The ridge that separates the front, right-hand portion from the middle of the green, can be used as a backstop against the prevailing breeze. Any shot either long, or left, of this ridge will leave golfers with a slippery, left-to-right downhill putt that is notoriously difficult to finish short of the hole. The middle portion of the green slopes significantly from back to front. Having your ball positioned below the pin is your best, and usually, only chance of one-putting this green. The green's back, left-hand portion can be accessed by landing the ball directly in this part of the green, or by hitting a right-to-left shot that lands in the centre of the green and 'feeds' across the ridge. However, as the hole is usually played into the wind, most approach shots land well short, and right, of the intended target. Over the years, I've endured my share of lengthy putts from the front, right of the green—with as much as eight feet of right-to-left break—to a back, left-hand flagstick. The particular challenge presented by this scenario, in part, helps explains why the hole rarely yields par.

Perhaps more than most holes, the outcome of your tee-shot on the seventeenth hole critically determines your next shot. On this difficult hole, recording a bogey five is a most respectable score, and, indeed, many of my matches have been decided on the seventeenth green with this score.

Casey O'Callaghan Golf Course Design, Inc.
Costa Mesa, California, USA

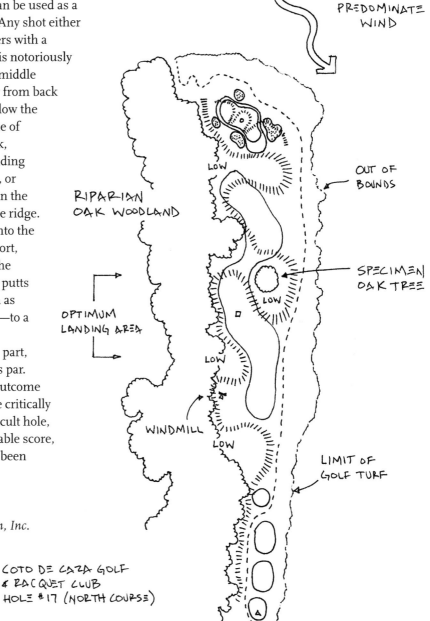

PREDOMINATE WIND

OUT OF BOUNDS

RIPARIAN OAK WOODLAND

SPECIMEN OAK TREE

LOW

LOW

OPTIMUM LANDING AREA

LOW

LOW

WINDMILL

LOW

LIMIT OF GOLF TURF

COTO DE CAZA GOLF
& RACQUET CLUB
HOLE #17 (NORTH COURSE)

ABOVE Shinnecock Hills Golf Club: Twelfth hole, USA. (Photo by Larry Lambrecht, LC Lambrecht Photography.)

BELOW Royal Montreal Golf Club (Blue): Sixteenth hole, Canada. (Photo by Tony Roberts, Tony Roberts Photography.)

OPPOSITE ABOVE Spyglass Hill Golf Course: Fourth hole, USA. (Photo by Tony Roberts, Tony Roberts Photography.)

OPPOSITE BELOW Pine Valley Golf Club: First hole, USA. (Photo by Tony Roberts, Tony Roberts Photography.)

ABOVE Pebble Beach Golf Links: Seventh hole, USA.
(Photos by Tony Roberts, Tony Roberts Photography.)

OPPOSITE ABOVE Pebble Beach Golf Links: Seventh hole, USA.
(Photos by Tony Roberts, Tony Roberts Photography.)

OPPOSITE BELOW Oakmont Country Club: Eighteenth hole, USA.
(Photo by Mark Whitright, Johnson Design Golf Marketing.)

Favourite Holes

Jack Snyder

Par-3s:
8th Mountain Shadows, USA
13th The Phoenician, USA
4th Las Montanas, USA
12th The Hideout, USA
18th Wailea (Blue), USA

Par-4s:
6th Wailea (Orange), USA NLE
9th Wailea (Orange), USA NLE
6th Concho Valley, USA
18th Oakmont, USA
4th The Hideout, USA

Par-5s:
12th Oakmont, USA
18th Sea Mountain, USA
13th The Hideout, USA
7th Legend Trail, USA
4th Wailea (Blue), USA

Robin Hiseman

Par-3s:
8th Cathcart Castle, Scotland
17th The Vintage Club (Mountain), USA
16th Ballybunion (Cashen), Ireland
6th Painswick, England
17th Hilton Park, Scotland

Par-4s:
11th Ballybunion (Old), Ireland
17th Deeside, Scotland
6th Kingsbarns, Scotland
10th Riviera, USA
5th Crystal Downs, USA

Par-5s:
13th Cruden Bay, Scotland
13th Royal Dornoch (Struie), Scotland
15th Ballybunion (Cashen), Ireland
1st Devil's Pulpit, Canada
1st Tobacco Road, USA

Neil Crafter

Par-3s:
15th Cypress Point Club, USA
5th Royal Melbourne (West), Australia
16th Royal Melbourne (East), Australia
10th Kingston Heath, Australia
15th North Berwick (West), Scotland

Par-4s:
3rd Royal Adelaide, Australia
2nd Glenelg, Australia
10th Royal Melbourne (West), Australia
17th Royal Melbourne (West), Australia
11th Cypress Point Club, USA

Par-5s:
2nd Kooyonga, Australia
5th Cypress Point Club, USA
6th Cruden Bay, Scotland
10th Royal Melbourne (East), Australia
9th San Francisco, USA

Gil Hanse

Par-3s:
5th Fishers Island, USA
17th Sand Hills, USA
4th National Golf Links of America, USA
11th Shinnecock Hills, USA
13th Muirfield, Scotland

Par-4s:
13th Pacific Dunes, USA
9th Cypress Point Club, USA
11th Pine Valley, USA
16th St. Andrews (Old Course), Scotland
5th Boston, USA

Par-5s:
4th Ridgewood (West), USA
13th Rustic Canyon, USA
14th Sand Hills, USA
6th Western Gailes, Scotland
3rd Prestwick, Scotland

Tim Lobb

Par-3s:
5th Royal Melbourne (West), Australia
9th Royal Lytham & St. Annes, England
10th Kingston Heath, Australia
15th Kingston Heath, Australia
15th Carton House (O'Meara), Ireland

Par-4s:
11th Wentworth (West), England
13th Royal County Down, Northern Ireland
18th Valderrama, Spain
18th Royal Lytham & St. Annes, England
6th Royal Melbourne (West), Australia

Par-5s:
6th Carnoustie, Scotland
7th Woburn (Marquess), England
17th Royal Melbourne (East), Australia
17th Royal Birkdale, England
14th Carton House (O'Meara), Ireland

David McLay Kidd

Par-3s:
15th North Berwick (West), Scotland
3rd Mauna Kea, USA
16th Cypress Point Club, USA
6th Queenwood, England
14th Royal Portrush (Dunluce),
　　Northern Ireland

Par-4s:
1st Machrihanish, Scotland
5th Bandon Dunes, USA
13th Gleneagles (Kings), Scotland
17th St. Andrews (Old Course), Scotland
8th Pebble Beach, USA

Par-5s:
13th Sand Hills, USA
18th Pacific Dunes, USA
13th Nanea, USA
9th Royal County Down, Northern Ireland
13th Augusta National, USA

Tom Doak

Par-3s:
4th Cruden Bay, Scotland
4th National Golf Links of America, USA
7th San Francisco, USA
11th St. Andrews (Old Course), Scotland
16th Cypress Point Club, USA

Par-4s:
6th Pacific Dunes, USA
13th North Berwick (West), Scotland
13th Pine Valley, USA
14th Royal Dornoch, Scotland
2nd St. Andrews (Old Course), Scotland

Par-5s:
4th Royal Melbourne (West), Australia
8th Royal West Norfolk, England
8th Crystal Downs, USA
13th Augusta National, USA
14th St. Andrews (Old Course), Scotland

Ross Perrett

Par-3s:
13th Barwon Heads, Australia
6th New South Wales, Australia
7th The National (Old), Australia
15th Kingston Heath, Australia
10th Moonah Links (Legends), Australia

Par-4s:
18th St. Andrews (Old Course), Scotland
3rd Royal Melbourne (West), Australia
11th Ballybunion (Old), Ireland
15th Victoria, Australia
9th Royal County Down, Northern Ireland

Par-5s:
4th Royal Melbourne (West), Australia
14th St. Andrews (Old Course), Scotland
1st The National (Ocean), Australia
9th Moonah Links (Legends), Australia
8th Metropolitan, Australia

Peter Fjallman

Par-3s:
4th Royal County Down, Northern Ireland
11th St. Andrews (Old Course), Scotland
12th Wallasey, England
16th Halmstad (North), Sweden
14th Royal Portrush (Dunluce),
　　Northern Ireland

Par-4s:
4th Woking, England
1st Machrihanish, Scotland
6th Machrie, Scotland
16th Pasatiempo, USA
17th St. Andrews (Old Course), Scotland

Par-5s:
13th Augusta National, USA
3rd Royal Liverpool, England
4th Valderrama, Spain
12th Kingsbarns, Scotland
14th St. Andrews (Old Course), Scotland

Scot Sherman

Par-3s:
3rd The Kittansett Club, USA
8th Kapalua (Plantation), USA
17th Mid-Ocean, Bermuda
15th Cypress Point Club, USA
16th Ponte Vedra Club (Ocean), USA

Par-4s:
8th Olde Farm, USA
8th Prairie Dunes, USA
10th Riviera, USA
17th National Golf Links of America, USA
17th St. Andrews (Old Course), Scotland

Par-5s:
4th Glen Mills, USA
5th Holston Hills, USA
11th TPC at Sawgrass, USA
15th Harbour Town, USA
16th Pinehurst (No. 2), USA

Bob Harrison

Par-3s:
12th Augusta National, USA
5th Royal Melbourne (West), Australia
15th Kingston Heath, Australia
9th Doonbeg, Ireland
7th Nirwana Bali, Indonesia

Par-4s:
13th North Berwick (West), Scotland
17th St. Andrews (Old Course), Scotland
14th New South Wales, Australia
11th The National (Moonah), Australia
17th Cypress Point Club, USA

Par-5s:
13th Augusta National, USA
4th Royal Melbourne (West), Australia
14th St. Andrews (Old Course), Scotland
9th Ellerston, Australia
9th Muirfield, Scotland

Todd Eckenrode

Par-3s:
11th Shinnecock Hills, USA
7th Pebble Beach, USA
4th Valley Club, USA
15th Pasatiempo, USA
14th Royal Portrush (Dunluce),
  Northern Ireland

Par-4s:
10th Riviera, USA
13th Cypress Point Club, USA
14th Barona Creek, USA
17th St. Andrews (Old Course), Scotland
13th Royal County Down, Northern Ireland

Par-5s:
16th Shinnecock Hills, USA
18th Pebble Beach, USA
1st Royal County Down, Northern Ireland
9th Monterey Peninsula (Dunes), USA
13th Augusta National, USA

Donald Knott

Par-3s:
5th Lahinch, Ireland
16th Cypress Point Club, USA
10th Spring City Resort (Lake), China
4th National Golf Links of America, USA
4th The National (Old), Australia

Par-4s:
4th Spyglass Hill, USA
11th Ballybunion (Old), Ireland
12th Pine Valley, USA
17th Royal Dornoch, Scotland
15th Prestwick, Scotland

Par-5s:
14th Spanish Bay, USA
16th Shinnecock Hills, USA
9th The Country Club, USA
15th Princeville (Prince), USA
16th Ballybunion (Old), Ireland

Phil Jacobs

Par-3s:
9th Ria Bintan, Indonesia
13th Lost City, South Africa
11th The Links, South Africa
2nd Durban, South Africa
5th Lahinch, Ireland.

Par-4s:
12th The Links, South Africa
6th The Cascades, Egypt
6th Erinvale, South Africa
8th Gary Player, South Africa
18th St Andrews (Old Course), Scotland

Par-5s:
11th Outeniqua (Fancourt), South Africa
7th Ria Bintan, Indonesia
3rd Durban, South Africa
16th The Links, South Africa
4th Lahinch, Ireland

Kyle Phillips

Par-3s:
16th Cypress Point Club, USA
8th Royal Troon, Scotland
13th The Grove, USA
15th Kingsbarns, Scotland
11th Robert Trent Jones, USA

Par-4s:
17th Cypress Point Club, USA
16th Dundonald, Scotland
6th Kingsbarns, Scotland
17th St. Andrews (Old Course), Scotland
6th Royal Haagsche, The Netherlands

Par-5s:
13th Augusta National, USA
18th Pebble Beach, USA
12th Kingsbarns, Scotland
14th Carnoustie, Scotland
6th Cruden Bay, Scotland

Harley Kruse

Par-3s:
5th Royal Melbourne (West), Australia
11th St. Andrews (Old Course), Scotland
8th Ballybunion (Old), Ireland
16th Cypress Point Club, USA
15th Kingston Heath, Australia

Par-4s:
3rd Royal Melbourne (West), Australia
6th Royal Melbourne (West), Australia
14th Royal Dornoch, Scotland
17th St. Andrews (Old Course), Scotland
3rd Royal County Down, Northern Ireland

Par-5s:
4th Royal Melbourne (West), Australia
14th St. Andrews (Old Course), Scotland
2nd The National (Moonah), Australia
5th New South Wales, Australia
7th Pine Valley, USA

Brett Mogg

Par-3s:
15th Kingston Heath, Australia
15th Shan Shui, Malaysia
15th Cypress Point Club, USA
5th Lahinch, Ireland
16th Warren, Singapore

Par-4s:
3rd Kingston Heath, Australia
11th Ballybunion (Old), Ireland
9th Suzhou Sun Island, China
6th Royal Melbourne (West), Australia
10th Riviera, USA

Par-5s:
5th Shan Shui, Malaysia
7th Kingston Heath, Australia
18th Mimosa (Mountainview), Philippines
18th Pebble Beach, USA
17th Macquarie Links International, Australia

Simon Gidman

Par-3s:
7th Rye, England
11th Royal Liverpool, England
8th Royal Troon, Scotland
8th Maidstone, USA
13th Swinley Forest, England

Par-4s:
12th Shinnecock Hills, USA
5th Royal County Down, Northern Ireland
18th Sunningdale (Old), England
18th St. Andrews (Old Course), Scotland
11th Merion (East), USA

Par-5s:
14th St. Andrews (Old Course), Scotland
1st The Berkshire (Red), England
9th Woodhall Spa, England
13th Augusta National, USA
2nd Southport & Ainsdale, England

Cal Olson

Par-3s:
15th Cypress Point Club, USA
16th Cypress Point Club, USA
7th Pebble Beach, USA
8th Coyote Hills, USA
3rd Aviara, USA

Par-4s:
8th Pebble Beach, USA
17th Cypress Point Club, USA
18th Coyote Hills, USA
17th St. Andrews (Old Course), Scotland
1st Pinehurst (No. 2), USA

Par-5s:
18th Pebble Beach, USA
18th Mission Hills, USA
16th Pinehurst (No. 2), USA
8th Aviara, USA
5th Cypress Point Club, USA

Michael Clayton

Par-3s:
5th Royal Melbourne (West), Australia
15th Kingston Heath, Australia
17th Sand Hills, USA
8th Royal Troon, Scotland
15th Portmarnock, Ireland
Par-4s:
10th Royal Melbourne (West), Australia
13th Portsea, Australia
6th Royal Melbourne (West), Australia
17th St. Andrews (Old Course), Scotland
18th Sand Hills, USA
Par-5s:
14th St. Andrews (Old Course), Scotland
12th Kingston Heath, Australia
14th Barnbougle Dunes, Australia
16th Shinnecock Hills, USA
4th Royal Melbourne (West), Australia

Steve Smyers

Par-3s:
5th Royal Melbourne (West), Australia
15th North Berwick (West), Scotland
15th Kingston Heath, Australia
16th Cypress Point Club, USA
10th Pacific Dunes, USA
Par-4s:
1st Pine Valley, USA
17th St. Andrews (Old Course), Scotland
14th Royal Dornoch, Scotland
5th Pinehurst (No. 2), USA
16th Turnberry (Ailsa), Scotland
Par-5s:
13th Augusta National, USA
15th Pine Valley, USA
3rd Old Memorial, USA
16th Ballybunion (Old), Ireland
18th Pebble Beach, USA

Dr Martin Hawtree

Par-3s:
5th Royal Melbourne (West), Australia
8th St. George's Hill, England
8th Royal Aberdeen, Scotland
15th Portmarnock, Ireland
16th Royal Melbourne (East), Australia
Par-4s:
1st Golf de Fontainebleau, France
1st Utrechtse 'De Pan,' The Netherlands
7th County Sligo, Ireland
15th Burnham & Berrow, England
18th Leven Links, Scotland
Par-5s:
1st Royal County Down, Northern Ireland
4th Royal Melbourne (West), Australia
5th Muirfield, Scotland
15th The Island, Ireland
15th Royal Birkdale, England

Bob Shearer

Par-3s:
15th Kingston Heath, Australia
16th Royal Melbourne (West), Australia
17th Jinmen Loch, China
12th Southern, Australia
12th Royal Birkdale, England
Par-4s:
14th Royal St. David's, Wales
6th Royal Melbourne (West), Australia
4th Woodlands, Australia
3rd Royal Adelaide, Australia
6th Jinmen Loch, China
Par-5s:
18th The Australian, Australia
4th Southern, Australia
4th Jinmen Loch, China
14th St. Andrews (Old Course), Scotland
18th Royal County Down, Northern Ireland

Jeff Howes

Par-3s:
4th Banff Springs, Canada
5th Gowran Park, Ireland
15th Cypress Point Club, USA
16th Cypress Point Club, USA
15th Ballybunion (Old), Ireland
Par-4s:
6th GC Adamstal, Austria
4th Gowran Park, Ireland
11th The Heritage, Ireland
10th Riviera, USA
11th Ballybunion (Old), Ireland
Par-5s:
3rd GC Adamstal, Austria
8th The Heritage, Ireland
18th Fota Island, Ireland
13th Augusta National, USA
10th Mt. Juliet, Ireland

Jeffrey D. Brauer

Par-3s:
16th Cypress Point Club, USA
5th Lahinch, Ireland
11th Los Angeles (North), USA
5th Royal Melbourne (West), Australia
7th Langdon Farms, USA
Par-4s:
8th Pebble Beach, USA
11th Shoreacres, USA
2nd San Francisco, USA
4th Royal St. George's, England
14th Gleneagles (Kings), Scotland
Par-5s:
4th Oakmont, USA
11th Devil's Pulpit, Canada
17th Royal Melbourne (East), Australia
12th Stonebridge Ranch (Dye), USA
11th Tobacco Road, USA

Jeremy Glenn

Par-3s:
16th Cypress Point Club, USA
17th TPC at Sawgrass, USA
12th Augusta National, USA
4th Banff Springs, Canada
10th Pine Valley, USA

Par-4s:
13th North Berwick (West), Scotland
14th Royal Dornoch, Scotland
10th Riviera, USA
11th Ballybunion (Old), Ireland
16th Royal Montreal (Blue), Canada
Par-5s:
13th Augusta National, USA
14th St. Andrews (Old Course), Scotland
4th World Woods (Pine Barrens), USA
18th Pebble Beach, USA
14th Royal Montreal (Red), Canada

Ian Scott-Taylor

Par-3s:
1st Royal Lytham & St Annes, England
17th Davyhulme Park, England
4th Baltusrol (Lower), USA
8th Royal Troon, Scotland
7th Pebble Beach, USA
Par-4s:
16th Merion (East), USA
12th Royal St. David's, Wales
12th Royal Liverpool, England
2nd Newport, USA
1st Holyhead, Wales
Par-5s:
18th National Golf Links of America, USA
11th Worplesdon, England
14th St. Andrews (Old Course), Scotland
13th Portmarnock, Ireland
12th Holyhead, Wales

Martin Ebert

Par-3s:
4th Victoria, Sri Lanka
5th Royal Worlington and Newmarket, England
7th Rye, England
10th Pine Valley, USA
14th Royal Portrush (Dunluce),
  Northern Ireland
Par-4s:
4th Rye, England
15th Enniscrone, Ireland
17th Skibo Castle, Scotland
17th St. Andrews (Old Course), Scotland
18th Rye, England
Par-5s:
2nd Royal Aberdeen, Scotland
8th Royal West Norfolk, England
14th Royal St. George's, England
14th St. Andrews (Old Course), Scotland
18th Royal County Down, Northern Ireland

Michael Cocking

Par-3s:
11th Yarra Yarra, Australia
11th St. Andrews (Old Course), Scotland
5th Royal Melbourne (West), Australia
15th Kingston Heath, Australia
8th Royal Troon, Scotland
Par-4s:
16th Commonwealth, Australia
17th Paraparaumu Beach, New Zealand
16th St. Andrews (Old Course), Scotland
10th Royal Melbourne (West), Australia
15th Victoria, Australia

Par-5s:
14th St. Andrews (Old Course), Scotland
12th Kingston Heath, Australia
17th Muirfield, Scotland
15th Woodlands, Australia
4th Royal Melbourne (West), Australia

Mike DeVries
Par-3s:
15th Cypress Point Club, USA
14th Maidstone, USA
10th Prairie Dunes, USA
17th Sand Hills, USA
15th North Berwick (West), Scotland
Par-4s:
4th Royal Dornoch, Scotland
11th Shore Acres, USA
17th St. Andrews (Old Course), Scotland
13th Pine Valley, USA
6th Crystal Downs, USA
Par-5s:
8th Crystal Downs, USA
6th Western Gailes, Scotland
13th Augusta National, USA
11th Lawsonia Links, USA
9th San Francisco, USA

Niall Glen
Par-3s:
17th Loch Lomond, Scotland
3rd Portstewart, Northern Ireland
9th Küssnacht Am Rigi, Switzerland
12th Mirage City, Egypt
14th Royal Tanger, Morocco
Par-4s:
9th Royal Aberdeen, Scotland
8th Emirates, United Arab Emirates
7th Doha, Qatar
4th Jebel Ali Hotel, United Arab Emirates
12th Ybrig, Switzerland
Par-5s:
6th Loch Lomond, Scotland
17th Valderamma, Spain
11th Maison Blanche, France
18th Abu-Dhabi, United Arab Emirates
18th Donnersberg, Germany

Thomas Himmel
Par-3s:
15th Cypress Point Club, USA
6th Tobacco Road, USA
8th Banff Springs, Canada
4th Royal County Down, Northern Ireland
5th Teeth of the Dog, Dominican Republic
Par-4s:
17th St. Andrews (Old Course), Scotland
8th Pebble Beach, USA
5th Cuscowilla, USA
18th True Blue, USA
13th Cuscowilla, USA
Par-5s:
14th St. Andrews (Old Course), Scotland
12th Kingsbarns, Scotland
18th Pebble Beach, USA
7th Pine Valley, USA
11th Tobacco Road, USA

Paul Daley
Par-3s:
6th New South Wales, Australia
16th Royal Melbourne (East), Australia
5th Royal Melbourne (West), Australia
15th Kingston Heath, Australia
5th Woodlands, Australia
Par-4s:
6th Royal Melbourne (West), Australia
5th Yarra Yarra, Australia
11th Commonwealth, Australia
10th Royal Melbourne (West), Australia
4th Barnbougle Dunes, Australia
Par-5s:
14th Kingston Heath, Australia
9th Muirfield, Scotland
6th Huntingdale, Australia
14th The Lakes, Australia
17th Victoria, Australia

Hisamitsu Ohnishi
Par-3s:
12th Augusta National, USA
12th Muirfield Village, USA
16th Augusta National, USA
7th Hirono, Japan
3rd The Cypress, Japan
Par-4s:
17th Cypress Point Club, USA
14th Muirfield Village, USA
17th Oharai, Japan
4th Hirono, Japan
15th The Cypress, Japan
Par-5s:
13th Augusta National, USA
18th Pebble Beach, USA
15th Muirfield Village, USA
15th Hirono, Japan
15th Oharai, Japan

Dr Michael Hurdzan
Par-3s:
5th Lahinch, Ireland
15th Cypress Point Club, USA
16th Cypress Point Club, USA
17th TPC Sawgrass, USA
13th Devil's Paintbrush, Canada
Par-4s:
11th Ballybunion (Old), Ireland
17th St. Andrews (Old Course), Scotland
13th Paraparaumu Beach, New Zealand
5th Royal Dornoch, Scotland
13th Royal Portrush (Dunluce),
   Northern Ireland
Par-5s:
12th Machrihanish, Scotland
5th New South Wales, Australia
7th Pine Valley, USA
4th Lahinch, Ireland
8th Devil's Pulpit, Canada

Michael Wolveridge
Par-3s:
7th Pebble Beach, USA
15th Cypress Point Club, USA
11th St. Andrews (Old Course), Scotland
14th The National (Ocean), Australia
16th Augusta National, USA
Par-4s:
8th Pebble Beach, USA
17th St. Andrews (Old Course), Scotland
14th Royal Dornoch, Scotland
4th Spyglass Hill, USA
Par-5s:
13th Moonah Links, Australia
18th Hope Island, Australia
13th Augusta National, USA
17th The National (Ocean), Australia
4th Royal Melbourne (West), Australia

Ronald Fream
Par-3s:
4th Golf Tabarka, Tunisia
14th Oulu, Finland
16th Cypress Point Club, USA
8th Redhawk, USA
2nd Hyatt Saujana Resort (Palm), Malaysia
Par-4s:
8th Pebble Beach, USA
10th Shore Gate, USA
6th Seminole, USA
14th Sentosa (Serapong), Singapore
14th Sparrebosch, South Africa
Par-5s:
4th Himalayan, Nepal
3rd Bonari Kogen, Japan
9th Desert Falls, USA
18th Nine Bridges, South Korea
9th Shore Gate, USA

Brian Phillips
Par-3s:
8th Sunningdale (Old), England
17th Sand Hills, USA
15th North Berwick (West), Scotland
6th Turnberry (Ailsa), Scotland
8th Royal Aberdeen, Scotland
Par-4s:
13th Pine Valley, USA
8th Woking, England
1st St. Andrews (Reverse Old Course), Scotland
5th Royal Dornoch, Scotland
6th Kingsbarns, Scotland
Par-5s:
9th North Berwick (West), Scotland
14th St. Andrews (Old Course), Scotland
11th Worlpesdon, England
1st Sand Hills, USA
12th Royal Porthcawl, Wales

Graeme Grant
Par-3s:
15th Cypress Point Club, USA
7th Pebble Beach, USA
15th Kingston Heath, Australia
16th Royal Melbourne (East), Australia
6th Links Lady Bay, Australia

Par-4s:
11th Merion (East), USA
3rd Royal County Down, Northern Ireland
4th Woodlands, Australia
9th Royal Melbourne (East), Australia
8th Kooyonga, Australia
Par-5s:
7th Pine Valley, USA
14th St. Andrews (Old Course), Scotland
15th Woodlands, Australia
10th Royal Melbourne (East), Australia
11th The Lakes, Australia

Josh Taylor
Par-3s:
12th Augusta National, USA
16th Cypress Point Club, USA
15th Kingston Heath, Australia
5th Royal Melbourne (West), Australia
6th Royal Dornoch, Scotland
Par-4s:
14th New South Wales, Australia
17th St. Andrews (Old Course), Scotland
10th Riviera, USA
9th Cypress Point Club, USA
6th Royal Melbourne (West), Australia
Par-5s:
13th Augusta National, USA
11th The Lakes, Australia
18th Kapalua (Plantation), USA
2nd Talking Stick (North), USA
14th St. Andrews (Old Course), Scotland

Thomas McBroom
Par-3s:
15th Royal St. Kitts, West Indies
17th Crowbush Cove, Canada
8th Rocky Crest, Canada
16th Beacon Hall, Canada
13th Heron Point, Canada
Par-4s:
2nd St. George's, Canada
2nd Lake Joseph, Canada
18th Le Géant, Canada
11th Deerhurst Highlands, Canada
10th Öviinbyrd, Canada
Par-5s:
15th Kytäjä (Lakeside), Finland
17th Morgan Creek, Canada
13th The Algonquin, Canada
9th Domaine Laforest, Canada
18th Deer Ridge, Canada

Peter Williams
Par-3s:
7th Pebble Beach, USA
10th Pine Valley, USA
16th Royal Melbourne (West), Australia
8th Royal Troon, Scotland
11th Yarra Yarra, Australia
Par-4s:
17th Cypress Point Club, USA
16th Royal Birkdale, England
17th Royal Lytham & St Annes, England
6th Seminole, USA
3rd Royal Melbourne (East), Australia

Par-5:
13th Augusta National, USA
15th Augusta National, USA
9th Muirfield, Scotland
7th Royal St. George's, England
14th St. Andrews (Old Course), Scotland

Brian Schneider
Par-3s:
16th Cypress Point Club, USA
5th Pine Valley, USA
7th Barnbougle Dunes, Australia
15th North Berwick (West), Scotland
15th Kingston Heath, Australia
Par-4s:
3rd National Golf Links of America, USA
13th Pine Valley, USA
12th St. Andrews (Old Course), Scotland
11th Ballybunion (Old), Ireland
12th The Addington, England
Par-5s:
16th Sand Hills, USA
4th Royal Melbourne (West), Australia
5th Shinnecock Hills, USA
14th St. Andrews (Old Course), Scotland
9th Muirfield, Scotland

Patrick Burton
Par-3s:
11th Pacific Dunes, USA
5th Lahinch, Ireland
15th Ballybunion (Old), Ireland
11th St. Andrews (Old Course), Scotland
14th Royal Portrush (Dunluce),
    Northern Ireland
Par-4s:
15th Prestwick, Scotland
9th Royal County Down, Northern Ireland
11th Ballybunion (Old), Ireland
14th Cruden Bay, Scotland
13th North Berwick (West), Scotland
Par-5s:
13th Pasatiempo, USA
16th Kingsbarns, Scotland
6th Western Gailes, Scotland
9th Royal Dornoch, Scotland
6th County Louth, Ireland

Kelly Blake Moran
Par-3s:
4th National Golf Links of America, USA
11th Shinnecock Hills, USA
17th Sand Hills, USA
3rd Moselem Springs, USA
11th St. Andrews (Old Course), Scotland
Par-4s:
4th Yale, USA
14th Garden City, USA
6th Shinnecock Hills, USA
10th Moselem Springs, USA
13th St. Andrews (Old Course), Scotland
Par-5s:
18th National Golf Links of America, USA
9th San Saba, USA
8th Boca Rio, USA
12th Royal Dornoch, Scotland
14th St. Andrews (Old Course), Scotland

Graham Papworth
Par-3s:
15th Cypress Point Club, USA
16th Cypress Point Club, USA
3rd Spyglass Hill, USA
7th Royal Melbourne (West), Australia
6th New South Wales, Australia
Par-4s:
9th Cypress Point Club, USA
17th Cypress Point Club, USA
10th Royal Melbourne (West), Australia
3rd Royal Adelaide, Australia
2nd The Vines (Lakes), Australia
Par-5s:
18th Palm Meadows, Australia
18th Harbour Town, USA
18th Pebble Beach, USA
5th New South Wales, Australia
13th Brookwater, Australia

Jeff Mingay
Par-3s:
3rd St. George's (Original 3rd), Canada
4th Riviera, USA
3rd Pine Valley, USA
6th National Golf Links of America, USA
6th Wolf Creek (South), Canada
Par-4s:
7th Inverness, USA
17th St. Andrews (Old Course), Scotland
5th Hamilton, Canada
17th Capilano, USA
16th Essex, Canada
Par-5s:
13th Augusta National, USA
8th Crystal Downs, USA
15th Blackhawk, Canada
7th Friar's Head, USA
11th TPC Sawgrass, USA

Jamie Dawson
Par-3s:
10th Kingston Heath, Australia
15th Kingston Heath, Australia
3rd Mauna Kea, USA
5th Royal Melbourne (West), Australia
7th Thirteenth Beach, Australia
Par-4s:
7th Jagorawi, Indonesia
6th Kapalua (Village), USA
5th Newcastle, Australia
9th Royal Canberra, Australia
6th Royal Melbourne (West), Australia
Par-5s:
16th Gungahlin Lakes, Australia
5th New South Wales, Australia
18th Royal Canberra, Australia
17th Royal Melbourne (East), Australia
11th Thirteenth Beach, Australia

Robin Nelson
Par-3s:
5th Lahinch, Ireland
12th Mangilao, Guam
17th TPC at Sawgrass, USA
15th Cypress Point Club, USA
4th Royal County Down, Northern Ireland

Par-4s:
17th Cypress Point Club, USA
17th St. Andrews (Old Course), Scotland
15th Shan Shui, Malaysia
11th New Ewa Beach International, USA
2nd Royal County Down, Northern Ireland
Par-5s:
18th Mimosa (Mountainview), Philippines
9th The Dunes at Maui Lani, USA
18th Pebble Beach, USA
18th Ravenwood, USA
9th Tiara Melaka, Malaysia

Tom Mackenzie

Par-3s:
5th County Louth, Ireland
7th The Addington, England
7th Royal Porthcawl, Wales
8th Royal Troon, Scotland
11th Ashridge, England
Par-4s:
4th Royal Dornoch, Scotland
14th County Louth, Ireland
12th Hayling, England
16th Saunton (East), England
18th Essex, USA
Par-5s:
6th County Louth, Ireland
6th Western Gailes, Scotland
14th St. Andrews (Old Course), Scotland
14th Hayling, England
14th Woodhall Spa (Hotchkin), England

Richard Mandell

Par-3s:
15th North Berwick (West), Scotland
10th Winged Foot (West), USA
9th Pinehurst (No. 2), USA
17th TPC Sawgrass, USA
3rd Yeamans Hall, USA
Par-4s:
5th St. George's, Canada
4th Westchester (West), USA
5th Mid-Ocean, Bermuda
17th Brora, Scotland
17th Prestwick, Scotland
Par-5s:
4th Bethpage State Park (Black), USA
14th St. Andrews (Old Course), Scotland
7th National Golf Links of America, USA
16th Pinehurst (No. 2), USA
15th Baltimore (Five Farms), USA

James Wilcher

Par-3s:
17th Mudgee, Australia
6th New South Wales, Australia
16th Cypress Point Club, USA
12th Augusta National, USA
7th Pebble Beach, USA
Par-4s:
16th Royal County Down, Northern Ireland
17th St. Andrews (Old Course), Scotland
4th Spyglass Hill, USA
17th Durban, South Africa
13th Monash, Australia

Par-5s:
13th Augusta National, USA
5th New South Wales, Australia
14th The Lakes, Australia
11th Waterville, Ireland
13th Brookwater, Australia

Forrest Richardson

Par-3s:
15th Cypress Point Club, USA
16th Cypress Point Club, USA
5th Lahinch, Ireland
17th Pebble Beach, USA
3rd Ventana Canyon (Mountain), USA
Par-4s:
4th Spyglass Hill, USA
18th The Hideout, USA
1st St. Andrews (Old Course), Scotland
17th St. Andrews (Old Course), Scotland
18th St. Andrews (Old Course), Scotland
Par-5s:
18th Pebble Beach, USA
9th Oakmont, USA
12th Phantom Horse, USA
9th The Hideout, USA
16th Legend Trail, USA

Shunsuke Kato

Par-3s:
15th North Berwick (West), Scotland
5th Lahinch, Ireland
16th Hokkaido, Japan
15th Cypress Point Club, USA
7th Pebble Beach, USA
Par-4s:
11th Ballybunion (Old), Ireland
8th Royal Dornoch, Scotland
4th Royal St. George's, England
8th Pebble Beach, USA
18th Whistling Straits (Straits), USA
Par-5s:
13th Augusta National, USA
18th Tomson, China
18th Taiheiyo, Japan
4th Lahinch, Ireland
18th Setonaikai, Japan

Dana Fry

Par-3s:
16th Cypress Point Club, USA
12th Augusta National, USA
6th New South Wales, Australia
12th Royal Birkdale, England
5th Royal Melbourne (West), Australia
Par-4s:
9th Maidstone, USA
16th Merion (East), USA
18th Shinnecock Hills, USA
3rd Royal County Down, Northern Ireland
13th Pine Valley, USA
Par-5s:
13th Augusta National, USA
8th Devil's Paintbrush, Canada
17th Muirfield, Scotland
8th Crystal Downs, USA
17th Prairie Dunes, USA

Mark Thawley

Par-3s:
16th Cypress Point Club, USA
8th Royal Troon, Scotland
11th Shinnecock Hills, USA
6th National Golf Links of America, USA
6th Royal Dornoch, Scotland
Par-4s:
17th St. Andrews (Old Course), Scotland
9th Cypress Point Club, USA
17th Cypress Point Club, USA
10th Riviera, USA
14th Royal Dornoch, Scotland
Par-5s:
6th Carnoustie, Scotland
8th Crystal Downs, USA
18th National Golf Links of America, USA
6th Western Gailes, Scotland
3rd Fenway, USA

Ron Garl

Par-3s:
12th Augusta National, USA
12th Eaglebrooke, USA
15th North Berwick (West), Scotland
8th Royal Troon, Scotland
2nd Victoria Hills, USA
Par-4s:
11th Ballybunion (Old), Ireland
2nd Indian River Club, USA
11th Minocqua, USA
17th St. Andrews (Old Course), Scotland
14th Taboo, Canada
Par-5s:
13th Augusta National, USA
18th Fiddlesticks (Long Mean), USA
17th Money Hill, USA
9th Muirfield, Scotland
16th Shinnecock Hills, USA

Casey O'Callaghan

Par-3s:
7th Pebble Beach, USA
15th North Berwick (West), Scotland
13th Muirfield, Scotland
6th Riviera, USA
4th Coto de Caza (North), USA
Par-4s:
17th Coto de Caza (North), USA
10th Riviera, USA
14th Cruden Bay, Scotland
3rd Muirfield, Scotland
8th Pebble Beach, USA
Par-5s:
18th Arroyo Trabuco, USA
18th Pelican Hill (Ocean), USA
18th Pebble Beach, USA
7th Turnberry (Ailsa), Scotland
6th Western Gailes, Scotland

NLE – No longer exists

Glossary

Amen corner
Pertaining to Augusta National Golf Club, and a section of its course—eleventh, twelfth, and thirteenth holes.

Arroyo
A brook or stream. Also pertains to a gully.

Alps
The seventeenth hole at Prestwick, Scotland, so named after the huge hill that must be carried to reach the green. When golf architect, Charles Blair Macdonald, designed the National Golf Links of America, he named the third hole 'Alps' in honour of Prestwick's seventeenth.

Agronomy
The science of soil management and crop production

Batter-top
Change of grade line between differing gradients: the transition between a gently sloping grade and a steeper slope below.

Bailout zone
A 'safe' area designated for landing golf shots away from a penalising course feature—invariably, from a hazard.

Blind Pew
The name given to the fourth hole at Spyglass Hill Golf Course, USA.

Burn
Derived from Old Teutonic: *burna*; *burne*; *bournon*; and latter from the Old English words meaning spring, fountain, or river. More recently, it refers to a brook in the north of Britain, and the name for water hazards on UK links. Some famous golfing burns include: Swilcan (St. Andrews); Barry (Carnoustie); Wilson's (Turnberry); Bluidy (Cruden Bay), and Pow (Prestwick).

Cape
A 'cape' within a bunker: a finger-like projection/bay. Also the giant, sleepered-bunker famously known as 'Cape' at Royal North Devon Golf Club, England.

Church Pews
A large bunker punctuated by rows of grassy hummocks, situated between the third and fourth fairways at Oakmont Country Club, USA.

Cross-bunkers
Cross-bunkers lie across the fairway, and formations vary between horizontal and diagonal placement.

Dell
Hollow or valley that is sometimes wooded. Also refers to the 'blind' par-3, fifth hole at Lahinch in Ireland.

Fescue
Any grass of the genus *Festuca*. The fine-leafed variety is an especially important links grass species, while tall fescue is commonly used in the rough on American courses, and it has a coarse leaf.

Fissure
An opening: usually long and narrow made by splitting, cracking, or separation of parts.

Foxy
The name given to the fourteenth hole at Royal Dornoch Golf Club, Scotland.

Golden Age of golf-course design
Many of the world's finest courses were built during the first third of the twentieth century, but activity ground to a halt with the onset of the stock market crash, bank foreclosures, and the Great Depression. Some of the most admired architects of this Golden Age era were Alister Mackenzie, Donald Ross, Harry S. Colt, A.W. Tillinghast, Stanley Thompson, Tom Simpson, J.F. Abercromby, Herbert Fowler, William S. Flynn, Charles B. Macdonald, Charles H. Alison, George Thomas Jr., and Seth Raynor.

Gorse
Any spiny, yellow-flowered shrub of the genus *Ulex*.

Great Triumvirate
Between 1894 and 1914, three outstanding British golfers dominated the game by winning the Open Championship sixteen times. They were Harry Vardon (six), John H. Taylor (five), and James Braid (five).

Green
In earlier times, the 'Green' referred to the entire golf course. Progressively after 1900, it has come to signify the finely mown area at the end of each hole from where golfers putt.

Green complex
A collective term: refers to the actual putting green, plus its immediate surrounds.

Hazard
Strictly applied, the word pertains to three types of hazards, namely, sand bunkers, water hazards, and lateral water hazards. Applied loosely, the word may also refer to wind, structures, rough, or even an opponent.

Heathland
An area of flattish, uncultivated land with low shrubs.

Heroic
The term 'heroic' applies to a hole, or a particular shot, that provides golfers with an opportunity to carry an obstacle or hazard to gain a favourable fairway position, with the proviso that there is sufficient room to avoid making such a design feature mandatory.

Hillock
Small hill or mound.

Hummock
A hillock or knoll.

Kikuyu
Pennisetum clandestinum: an aggressive species of grass native to North East Africa, and Kenya. Under close cutting it forms a thick mat, and can keep out many weeds. Kikuyu stands up to wear but never produces a fine turf. Frequently found in warmer climates.

Klondyke
The par-5, fourth hole at Lahinch, Ireland, with its famously 'blind' second shot over a small rock inserted into the large hill that traverses the fairway. For many years prior to Martin Hawtree's upgrade at Lahinch, it was the fifth hole.

Landscape
A landscape: natural or imaginary scenery, as seen in a broad view.

Lay-up
A golfer's measred decision of selecting a club to lay-up short of trouble, invariably, from a hazard or broken ground.

Links
According to eminent geologist, Dr Robert Price, links are 'wind-blown sand landforms.' Typically, linksland is covered by the fine, robust, salt-resistant grass species, fescues and bents, along with the dune-binding grass species, such as, marram and sea-lyme. The noun *links* applies in the singular or plural form, and is derived from the thirteenth century Old English word, *hlinc*.

Massif
A compact group of mountain heights.

Old Course
Pertains to the Old Course at St. Andrews, Scotland. The Old Course continues to be the most celebrated and revered layout in golf, and it is home to the Royal and Ancient Golf Club.

Old Tom
Born: 16 June 1821. Died: 24 May 1908. 'Old' Tom Morris was an influential Keeper of the Green at St. Andrews, and won the Open championship four times. Morris designed and redesigned many early UK links.

Maxwell Rolls
US golf architect, Perry Maxwell, designed and built 'wild' and marvelously contouring greens: 'Maxwell Rolls.'

Palimpsest
Pertains to a piece of writing-material or manuscript where the original writing has been effaced to make room for other writing.

Penal
When the shot requirement is 'penal' there is an air of finality in the punishment it doles out to golfers who err in judgement, or shotmaking. Often, a lost ball, or a stroke(s) lost to par follows. One criticism of the 'penal' school of architecture is, that it doesn't matter to what degree a golfer errs; if they err slightly, the penalty is the same as for those who err greatly.

Pot-bunker
A tiny, steep-walled bunker, most commonly found at British links. Not infrequently, a golfer's recovery shot will be played out sideways, or backwards.

Postage Stamp
The eighth hole at Royal Troon, Scotland, is known as the 'Postage Stamp' in recognition of its diminutive and elusive green.

Punchbowl
A once, popular style of green that is small, lies in a depression, and is surrounded by banks. Unless situated upon sandy soil, prone to flooding.

Ravine
A deep, narrow gorge.

Redan
The par-3, fifteenth hole at North Berwick (West) in Scotland is known as 'Redan.' One of the most famous and copied holes in the golf world, it has distinct architectural features: the green lies along a ridge about 35-45 degrees set off from the line of play; there is a guarding front, left bunker with others stationed behind the green; and the slope of the green is front-to-back.

Restoration
The process of restoring/returning the golf course to its original designed state.

Riparian area
Home to a diverse group of plants and animals, the transitional zone between aquatic and terrestrial (or upland) environments, occurs as a belt along the banks of rivers, streams, and lakes. Riparian Area is derived from the Latin word *ripa* meaning streambank.

Road hole
The seventeenth hole at the Old Course, St. Andrews, so named because of the proximity of the right-hand side of the fairway, and its green, to the road running alongside the famous links. A pot-bunker adjoining the front left of the green is known as 'Road' bunker, and it has ruined many scores.

Routing
The configuration of holes in relation to the existing terrain and site parameters: the flow and sequence of holes on a site.

Sahara
Sahara bunker: a massive bunker on the seventeenth hole at Prestwick, Scotland, situated immediately after the Alps hill, and just short of the green. Sahara is also the card name of the second hole at the National Golf Links of America, USA, and the name of the third hole at Royal St. George's, England.

Scoonie
Scoonie hazard: an immense water hazard positioned in front of the eighteenth green at Leven Links, Scotland. The hole is also known as 'Scoonie.'

Shaper
The individual who interprets the architect's plans and shapes the land where needed. Large design firms may employ a team of shapers on any given course project.

Strath
A broad mountain valley; also pertains to 'Strath' bunker on the eleventh hole at the Old Course, St. Andrews.

Swale
An elongated hollow.

Tweaking
Altering the formal design on paper to make the course more functional. Tweaking may occur during the initial staking of the golf hole layout, during construction, or after construction. Tweaking is visibly noticed regarding the establishment of turf lines and setting maintenance guidelines.

Credits

PHOTOGRAPHIC CREDITS

Aidan Bradley: ix
Ronald Fream: 86; 87
Russell Kirk: 97
Larry Lambrecht: v; 60; 61; 94; 96; 116-17; 120-21; 138 (above)
Brett Mogg: 95
Nicholas Quin: Dustjacket (inside-right flap)
Tony Roberts: 138 (below); 139; 140; 141 (above)
David Scaletti: 16-17; 24-25; 44; 45; 46-47; 78-79; 82-83
Mark Whitright: 141 (below)

ILLUSTRATION CREDITS

Lyndon Cocking: 65
Michael Cocking: 73
Chris Cunningham: 13
Golf Publishing Limited: 11 (3-D Illustration)
Jane Hunter: 99
Barry King: Cover image; 41; 75
Meredith Liddle: 15
Glenn McCulloch: 101
Paul Mogford: 52
Anthony Oakshett: 63 (above)
Kyle Phillips: 89

ACKNOWLEDGMENTS

Congratulations to all the contributors for your excellent essays and illustrations. Working with you has been a spirited and most rewarding experience.

The vibrant images from professional photographers, namely, Aidan Bradley, Russell Kirk, Larry Lambrecht, Nicholas Quin, Tony Roberts, David Scaletti, and Mark Whitright, add an extra layer to the project. The photography provided by Ronald Fream and Brett Mogg is also most appreciated. Thank you to The Gleneagles Hotel, Scotland, for illustrations and photography of the Kings Course's thirteenth hole. Authored by John F. Morton II, *The Golf Courses of James Braid* (1996) by Grant Books, proved a valuable reference for David McLay Kidd's essay on 'Braid's Brawest.'

It is a pleasure to acknowledge Barry King, a local Melbourne artist and friend, whose wonderful painting of Augusta National's twelfth hole captures the essence of this book.

I'm grateful to the many club stewards who relayed information pertaining to the various golf holes. My thanks is also extended to Pebble Beach Company (PBC) for granting image reproduction rights of Pebble Beach Golf Links and of Spyglass Hill Course.

Australians Neil Crafter and Paul Mogford annually produce *Golf Architecture*, the eagerly awaited Journal of the Society of Australian Golf Course Architects. It was in this publication (Issue 4, Dec. 2000), that Bob Shearer's essay on the eighteenth hole at The Australian Golf Club first appeared. Thank you to Paul Mogford of Urban Edge Landscape Architects, Melbourne, for your accompanying sketch of the hole.

Andrew Cunningham of Studio Pazzo draws praise for his stylish book design.

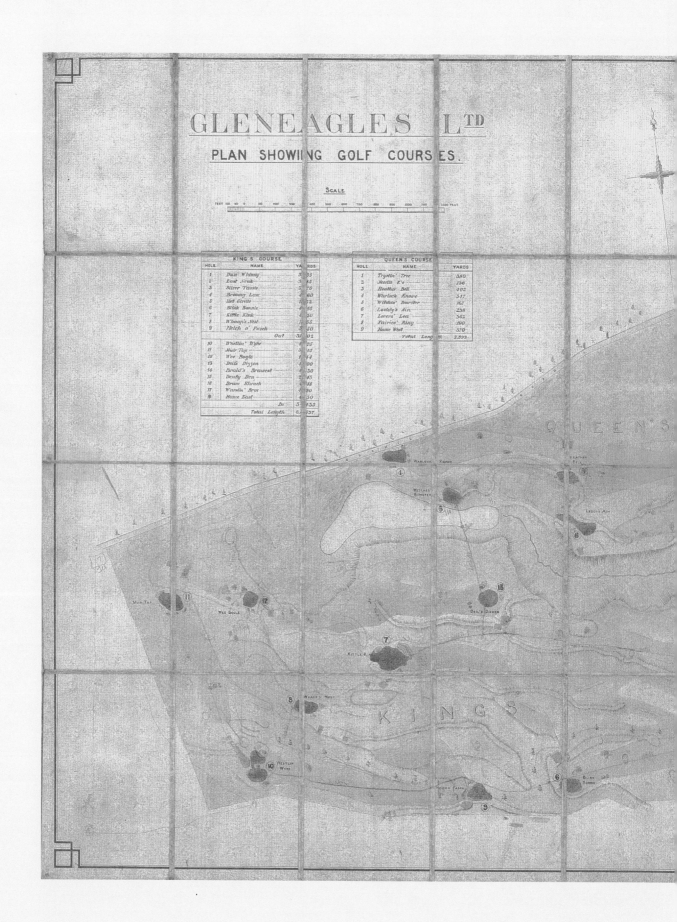

GLENEAGLES LTD

PLAN SHOWING GOLF COURSES.

Scale

KING'S COURSE		
HOLE	NAME	YARDS
1	Dun' Whinny	3
2	East Neuk	3
3	Silver Tassie	5
4	Broomy Law	4
5	Het Girdle	1
6	Blink Bonnie	4
7	Kittle Kink	4
8	Whaup's Nest	1
9	Heich o' Fash	3
	Out	3
10	Wrestlin' Nyln	4
11	Muir Tap	5
12	Wee Bogle	1
13	Deil's Ditzen	4
14	Braid's Bravest	4
15	Denty Den	2
16	Drum Sheuch	4
17	Warslin' Brae	4
18	Home East	4
	In	3
	Total Length	6

QUEEN'S COURSE		
HOLE	NAME	YARDS
1	Tryslin' Tree	380
2	Needle E'e	136
3	Heather Bell	402
4	Warlock Knowe	347
5	Witches' Bowster	167
6	Laichly's Ain	238
7	Lovers' Lea	542
8	Fairies' Ring	100
9	Hame West	570
	Total Length	2,592